Euthanasia for Death Duties

Euthanasia for Death Duties

Putting Inheritance Tax Out of Its Misery

BARRY BRACEWELL-MILNES

The Institute of Economic Affairs

First published in Great Britain in 2002 by
The Institute of Economic Affairs
2 Lord North Street
Westminster
London SW1P 3LB
in association with Profile Books Ltd

A CIP catalogue record for this book is available from the British Library.

ISBN 0 255 36513 6

Many IEA publications are translated into languages other than English or are
reprinted. Permission to translate or to reprint should be sought from the
General Director at the address above.

Typeset in Stone by MacGuru
info@macguru.org.uk

Printed and bound in Great Britain by Hobbs the Printers

CONTENTS

THE AUTHOR

Barry Bracewell-Milnes was sacked in 1973 by Mr Campbell Adamson, Director-General of the Confederation of British Industry (CBI), for supporting capitalism, free enterprise and the market economy.

Since leaving the CBI, he has worked for himself as author and consultant on economic and tax policy. Among other posts held he was Principal Scientific Collaborator, Erasmus University Rotterdam, 1973–8, and Economic Adviser, the Institute of Directors, 1973–96.

He is the author of some two dozen books in the field of economic and tax policy, including *The Measurement of Fiscal Policy: An Analysis of Tax Systems in Terms of the Political Distinction between 'Right' and 'Left'* (1971), *Is Capital Taxation Fair? The Tradition and the Truth* (1974), *Tax Avoidance and Evasion: The Individual and Society* (1979), *The Economics of International Tax Avoidance: Political Power versus Economic Law* (1980), *The Taxation of Industry: Fiscal Barriers to the Creation of Wealth* (1981). He has also written *Is a Mast a Must? How to Fight off Intruders* (2001) about a successful campaign against a telecommunications mast.

FOREWORD

From the early days of the Institute, its authors have been concerned about the burden of taxation. Governments have the unique ability to extract money from some people and to transfer it to others via various 'public interest' programmes, subject only to the constraints of periodic elections. Pressure groups which benefit from the spending programmes emerge and make tax reductions difficult. Indeed, in many countries tax burdens have been rising over the last century as well-intentioned, if misguided, 'social reformers' have identified new 'needs' which require finance from taxpayers.

One of the Institute's leading authors on tax reform is Dr Barry Bracewell-Milnes, who for many years has been applying the logic of economic analysis to the British tax system. In Research Monograph 54, he returns to inheritance tax.

At first sight, inheritance tax may seem a minor tax, of diminishing relative importance: it yields only about 1.5 per cent of Inland Revenue tax receipts, compared with about 19 per cent early last century. Nevertheless, it affects many people of fairly modest means. Since the threshold is at present only £242,000, people of such means who live in higher-price housing areas in Britain will find they have estates which attract tax at a 40 per cent rate.

Dr Bracewell-Milnes begins by setting out the traditional arguments against inheritance tax. For example, the administrative and compliance costs are exceptionally high; the Treasury may lose, on balance, from collecting death duties rather than the taxes that would have been levied had the revenues remained in taxpayers' hands; the tax imposes a disproportionately heavy burden on small and medium-sized business; and it shortens time horizons.

His concern, however, is primarily with the adverse effect of death duties on what he terms 'perpetual saving' – that is, saving that is never drawn down, whether or not it was initially planned to be perpetual (see especially Chapter 4 and Annex A to that chapter). He argues that the perpetual saver is a public benefactor because he or she provides the rest of the community with a permanent loan at rates chargeable for loans with maturity dates. The perpetual saver enjoys his abstinence from consumption and at the same time provides resources for the rest of society. A major problem with death duties is that they make saving in perpetuity more expensive for the testator and so '. . . must be expected to reduce the volume of such saving and the benefits it confers on society' (p. 59).

Bracewell-Milnes also attacks the case sometimes made that death duties are justified on the grounds that they promote 'equality'. The concept of 'equality' is elusive and measurement is difficult but, in addition to these problems, Bracewell-Milnes points out that a tax such as death duties, which reduces saving in perpetuity and therefore increases the spending of richer people, will actually *increase* the observed inequality of spending and lifestyles.

His conclusion is that inheritance tax does immense economic damage and is '. . . perverse and counterproductive for its own ostensible purposes, egalitarian or otherwise' (p. 94). Its abolition would be simple; its yield is small and might well be offset, after abolition, by increased yields from other taxes. It should, in Dr Bracewell-Milnes' words, be 'put out of its misery' (p. 94).

In summary, readers will find in Dr Bracewell-Milnes' paper not just the conventional listing of the pros and cons of death duties but also novel arguments, which governments would do well to note, about the dangers of reducing saving in perpetuity. As in all IEA papers, the views expressed are those of the author, not of the Institute (which has no corporate view), its managing trustees, Academic Advisory Council members or senior staff.

COLIN ROBINSON

Editorial Director, Institute of Economic Affairs
Professor of Economics, University of Surrey

SUMMARY

- A tax on giving or bequest always causes a social loss, and this social loss (or wealth destroyed) always at least equals the revenue yield.
- The social loss always exceeds the revenue yield, except in the limiting case.
- Thus, except in the limiting case, giving and inheritance have negative economic taxable capacity: the damage done by taxes on them exceeds the revenue they yield.
- Because the perpetual saver prefers the shadow of potential use to the substance of actual use, the rest of society enjoys a permanent loan at rates chargeable for loans with maturity dates.
- A tax on saving in perpetuity must be expected to reduce its supply: there are no countervailing influences. The rest of society loses as the saver in perpetuity shifts to spending.
- Capital prosperity can vary independently of income prosperity. Capital prosperity should be nurtured and cultivated, not neglected, damaged or destroyed.
- Inheritance tax cheapens the spending of the rich taxpayer relatively both to his own saving and to the saving and spending of the poor.
- Inheritance tax increases the inequality of spending and may increase inequality overall.

- The social background is more favourable than it has ever been to the abolition of inheritance tax.
- Inheritance tax does immense economic damage and is perverse and counterproductive for its own ostensible purposes, egalitarian or otherwise. It should be put out of its misery.

DIAGRAMS AND TABLES

Euthanasia for Death Duties

1 INTRODUCTION

The prince shall not take of the people's inheritance by oppression, to thrust them out of their possession.

EZEKIEL XLVI, 18

Inheritance tax is an impost of great antiquity. Inheritance taxation can be traced back through the medieval *heriot* or 'voluntary' donation from the tenant to his feudal lord to the Roman twentieth (5 per cent) or *vicesima hereditatium*[1] and ultimately to Egypt in the first millennium before Christ. The main reason for its persistence over such a long period was its convenience for governments: governments were inevitably involved in effecting the passage of title to the heirs of the deceased, and it was little extra trouble to levy a tax charge when the relevant facts were already at the government's disposal.

Estate duty or *capital transfer tax* is a tax on the testator or donor. *Legacy duty* or *succession duty* is usually a tax on the heir or donee. *Inheritance tax* is usually a tax on the heir or donee; but in the United Kingdom it is a tax on the testator or donor. *Death duties* is a generic term for any tax on the occasion of death and (by extension) on lifetime gifts (gifts *inter vivos*).

---

1   The spelling *hereditatium* is more correct than *hereditatum*, since it is found in inscriptions wherever the word is not abbreviated.

In the United Kingdom death duties were modernised (and increased) as estate duty by Sir William Harcourt in 1894. Capital transfer tax, with lifetime cumulation of *inter vivos* transfers, was introduced in 1975. Lifetime cumulation was reduced to ten-year cumulation in 1981. Capital transfer tax was replaced by inheritance tax in 1986. Ten-year cumulation was reduced to seven years. All these taxes were and are levied on the testator or donor.

In 2001/02 inheritance tax is levied at 40 per cent on the part of the deceased's estate exceeding £242,000. Inter-spousal transfers are exempt. Business assets as defined are also effectively exempt, since business property relief is granted at 100 per cent; agricultural property is relieved similarly. Business assets in this sense are primarily unquoted companies and other unquoted trading concerns and their associated assets; quoted shares held by individuals are excluded from the definition. There was a cross-party consensus in Parliament in favour of this effective exemption of business and agricultural property.

Death duties used to be serious revenue raisers. As recently as 1908/09 they provided 19 per cent of total Inland Revenue tax receipts; but this figure had fallen to some 1.6 per cent in 2000/01. The current yield is of the order of one penny on the basic rate of income tax. To put the same point differently, the yield of inheritance tax has for many years been a small proportion of the annual *increase* in total tax revenue (some 12.5 per cent in 2000)[2]: on this basis, the abolition of inheritance tax *for ever* could have been funded by a reduction of one-eighth in the *increase* in the government's budget in a single year. Inheritance tax is now part of the government's small change, and the reasons for keeping it on have

---

2   Financial Statement and Budget Report, March 2000, p. 203.

long ceased to be financial. The arguments for and against inheritance tax are social and political, arguments for and against inheritance.

Inheritance has a good Jewish and Christian background. There are some 130 references to inheritance in the King James Bible (Authorised Version), some material, some spiritual, some both, but all favourable.[3] Sustained criticism of the institution of inheritance, originating in the eighteenth century, was largely irreligious or anti-clerical in character, associated with the French Revolution, and partly utopian.[4] This line of thinking culminated in the introduction of the British estate duty by Sir William Harcourt in 1894 under the slogan 'we are all socialists now'.

One enduring theme in recent centuries has been that inheritance weakens the will or the obligation to work. 'Mr Strahan . . . observing that many men were kept back from trying their fortunes there [in London] because they were born to a competency, said, "Small certainties are the bane of men of talents", which Johnson confirmed.'[5] The trouble with this argument in the present context is that it exalts a commonplace to a prescription for policy. Men 'try their fortunes' when obliged to do so by poverty;

---

3   'The Lord hath taken you . . . to be unto him a people of inheritance, as ye are this day' (Deuteronomy iv, 20); 'The Lord knoweth the days of the upright: and their inheritance shall be for ever' (Psalm xxxvii, 18); 'Save thy people, and bless thine inheritance' (Psalm xxviii, 9), imitated in the Anglican Order for Morning Prayer of 1662: *Priest:* 'O Lord, save thy people.' *Answer:* 'And bless thine inheritance.'

4   Guido Erreygers, 'Views on Inheritance in the History of Economic Thought', in *Is Inheritance Legitimate? Ethical and Economic Aspects of Wealth Transfers* (ed. Erreygers and Toon Vandevelde, Springer Verlag, Berlin, 1997). Also Erreygers, *Early Socialist Thought on Bequest and Inheritance* (paper presented at the 1996 History of Economics Society Conference, University of British Columbia, Vancouver, Canada), mimeo, UFSIA, University of Antwerp, June 1996.

5   Boswell's *Life of Johnson*, 27 March 1775.

but they may be made more rather than less productive by the possession of independent means. David Hume and Edward Gibbon, for example, were not held back by being born to a competency. Enforced poverty may act as a spur to hard work; but that is not a good reason for making people poor. It is already possible in the United Kingdom for a testator with a puritanical disapproval of inheritance to disinherit his heirs; a general impoverishment of legatees through state action would not yield the optimal outcome.[6]

Apart from their unsuitability as a means of persuading people to work, death duties have attracted an increasing range of criticisms in recent years. It is argued against them that they are old-fashioned and form no logical part of a modern tax system; that their administrative and compliance costs are exceptionally high; that the Treasury may lose more than their nominal yield from the reductions they effect in the yields of other taxes; that they are a disproportionately heavy burden on small and medium-sized firms and that they thus increase unemployment, since these firms are principal providers of new jobs; that they cause damaging 'short-termist' distortions to the economy by artificially curtailing the time-horizons of economic agents; that they are unthrifty and anticipatory taxes that levy on the present value of future income flows; that the proceeds of taxes on capital are used to defray government spending on current account; and in general that they are inimical to the creation of material wealth in a capitalist system.

These arguments are correct and important, and I have ad-

---

6   Inheritance without taxation weakens the beneficiary's incentive to work (because the beneficiary is born to a competency) but increases his incentive to save (because saving is more attractive relatively to spending for the beneficiary as for the testator; the beneficiary will be a testator in his turn).

dressed them elsewhere.[7] Most of them constitute hidden costs and thus fall within our terms of reference here. The present monograph, however, focuses on the complementary and less familiar argument that death duties are no less damaging through their destruction of immaterial wealth, the wealth that subsists in the mind, and that they are perverse and counterproductive in terms of the redistributive purposes that now constitute their principal justification in the eyes of their supporters.

There is little reasoning in favour of death duties nowadays. In so far as they are still credited with a rationale, the case for retaining them appears to rest on one or more of the following arguments:

1 Death duties are levied on transfers and thus do not damage the productive economy. Under a transfer tax, what one party loses the other party gains. There is no loss to society.

2 Death duties fall only on the legatees, not on the legators. The legatees are receiving money for which they have not worked or saved: a tax on legatees is thus less painful than any other form of taxation.

3 Earning, spending and saving are taxed: it is right economically and socially that wealth should be taxed as well. The economically best and least painful method of taxing wealth is on death.

4 Death duties reduce the inequality of wealth and thus reduce inequality overall.

7 *Will to Succeed: Inheritance without Taxation* (Adam Smith Institute, London, 1994). The list of arguments against death duties is given in my 'The Hidden Costs of Inheritance Taxation', in *Is Inheritance Legitimate?*, op. cit. They are discussed further in Chapter 2.

This monograph shows that all these arguments are wrong on their own terms. If points (1) to (4) are merits, death duties are perverse and counterproductive in terms of all the purposes that their supporters wish them to serve.

2 WHERE THIS MONOGRAPH DIFFERS

There are arguments for and against death duties in many different, but interrelated, dimensions, including economics, ethics and equality. A number of the principal arguments against death duties (traditional, but increasingly important in recent years) are listed in the Introduction, and discussed briefly in this chapter. In order to keep the monograph to a reasonable length, I wish to concentrate on the arguments 1–4 outlined in the Introduction; most of them are not new (I have explained them in the works cited), but they have not been accepted into mainstream thinking, nor have they been deployed as they are in the present monograph.

The purpose of this chapter is to put these novelties into the context of the familiar by explaining their relationships with more traditional considerations.

Traditional criticisms of death duties

The arguments listed in the Introduction are briefly expanded here.

Death duties are no part of a logical tax system. Historical background is given on pp. 21–4 above.[1] For many centuries the

---

1   A more detailed account of the estate duty 1894–1965 is given in Chapter II of C. T. Sandford, *Taxing Inheritance and Capital Gains*, Hobart Paper 32, Institute of Economic Affairs, London, 1965.

principal argument in favour of death duties was that they were easy for the fisc to collect. In the nineteenth century egalitarian justifications became more important. Both types of argument seem dated now. It is widely recognised that most assets subject to death duties have been subject to tax during the testator's lifetime, so that death duties constitute a form of double, triple or other multiple taxation. The principal force keeping death duties in place is inertia. Few would argue for their introduction if they were not already part of the system.

The administrative and compliance costs of death duties are exceptionally high. Although the government is necessarily involved in the passage of title from the deceased to his heirs, this advantage may be outweighed by the requirement to value assets that change hands otherwise than by sale. This is a major compliance cost for the taxpayer. Litigated valuations may double or halve when a higher court adjudicates: this is the hazard of a tax that is not based on market transactions. Many non-taxpayers are obliged to spend time and money on valuations and other complexities merely in order to establish non-liability: the ratio of these non-taxpayers to taxpayers is high for death duties and perhaps higher than for any other tax.

The Treasury may lose rather than gain from death duties when second-round effects are taken into consideration. The Treasury gains from death duties the published figures of yield (minus costs of collection). However, that is only the immediate or first-round effect. If the yield of death duties had remained in the hands of the taxpayers, it would have been spent or stayed invested. The Treasury would have gained value-added tax, excise duties, pay-as-you-earn

income tax, national insurance contributions, corporation tax ...
On balance, the Treasury may lose rather than gain from death duties, so that it would gain rather than lose from their abolition.

*Death duties are a disproportionately heavy burden on small and
medium-sized firms.* Although business and agricultural property
reliefs effectively exempt qualifying property, the assets have to
qualify. If they do not, the burden is heaviest on small and
medium-sized firms, since the rate of tax is proportional above a
threshold that often fails to cover the value of the family home. Another category at risk is smaller non-business properties that are
an adornment to their neighbourhoods but have no claim to national status.

*Death duties cause damaging 'short-termist' distortions to the economy
by artificially curtailing the time-horizons of economic agents.* Death
duties make it rational for a testator to have a time-horizon termi-
nating with his death. Tax-free inheritance makes it rational for
him to look ahead for several generations and in principle without
limit. This longer perspective facilitates economic opportunities
that the shorter perspective obstructs or prevents.

*Death duties are unthrifty and anticipatory taxes that levy on the pre-
sent value of future income flows.* Adam Smith said: 'All taxes upon
the transference of property of every kind, so far as they diminish
the capital value of that property, tend to diminish the funds des-
tined for the maintenance of productive labour. They are all more
or less unthrifty taxes that increase the revenue of the sovereign,
which seldom maintains any but unproductive labourers, at the
expense of the capital of the people, which maintains none but

productive.'[2] Smith's concept of *unthriftiness* concerns the relative productivities of the government sector and the private sector. The related concept of *anticipation* concerns unthriftiness in another sense: death duties levy now on what the confiscated capital would otherwise have yielded in income tax, corporation tax, value added tax and other charges. In both senses, death duties kill the goose instead of taxing the eggs.

The proceeds of taxes on capital are used to defray government spending on current account. The yield of death duties constitutes Treasury funds like the yield of any other tax. The division between current and capital government spending is decided on other grounds.

Is giving a zero-sum game?

The traditional treatment of non-commercial money transfers is that they are zero-sum: what one party loses, the other gains. This approach has been followed both academically and in the national-income accounts and for gifts to both charities, individuals and corporate entities.

This method of proceeding confuses *financial exchange* with *economic exchange*. It is right for the former, which is trivial, and wrong for the latter, which is substantial.

If you spend £50 on groceries at a supermarket or elsewhere (or £50 million on buying a company), you pay out £50 and the other party receives £50. Financially, the transaction is truistically zero-sum: what one party gains, the other loses. But this is a misleading representation of economic truth. If you pay £50 for goods

---

2   *The Wealth of Nations*, Book v, Chapter ii, Appendix to Articles i and ii.

worth £50 to you, what is the point of the expedition to the supermarket? Why get the car out of the garage (and who pays for the car)? Why get out of bed? The point of the expedition is that the £50 of groceries are worth *more* to you than £50 by a margin large enough to defray the cost of your time and trouble and the cost of using the car and still leave enough 'profit' to make the expedition worthwhile. For example, the cost of the car may be £5 and the cost of your time and trouble £10, but the groceries may be worth £90 to you in the sense that you would if necessary pay £90 to have them rather than go without; so you have made a 'profit' (or consumer's surplus) of £25 (= £90 − 50 − 10 − 5). This consumer's profit is closely analogous to a commercial profit; indeed, the supermarket that sells the goods at £50 has a producer's surplus analogous to the consumer's surplus (the £50 exceeds an irreducible short-term minimum by enough to enable the supermarket to stay in business).

All this is familiar; but the academic and popular perceptions are that gifts and bequests are another country: they do things differently there.

In *The Wealth of Giving*[3] I sought to show that gifts and bequests are not mere zero-sum financial transfers, but acts of wealth creation like production and commercial exchange. A gift or bequest is a use of funds entirely competitive with spending and saving. It is the donor or testator who decides between the competing uses and destinations of the funds at his disposal (even though his judgment is influenced by what he knows about the recipient or potential recipient). A gift or bequest is made if and only

---

3   *The Wealth of Giving: Every One in His Inheritance*, Research Monograph 43, Institute of Economic Affairs, London, 1989.

if its value to the donor or testator exceeds the value of the funds to him in competing uses. This anchors the theory of giving in mainstream economics: all are parts of a single whole, and commercial and altruistic motives compete with each other on equal terms in the mind of the economic agent. It is very different from the traditional concept of the economic agent, whose generally commercial motivation is mysteriously modified and qualified by external notions of altruism. The principal difference is that in the traditional conception the donor or testator is financially the loser; in my conception, he is economically the gainer, since otherwise he would not part with his money without consideration.

The distinction between a financial exchange and an economic exchange may be illustrated not only by the difference between a tax payment on the one hand and a gift to a charity or an individual on the other, but also by the difference between gifts to different charities. The charitable sector is not monolithic. Although all charities must have enough in common to be acceptable to the Charities Commission, that is where the resemblance ends. I support charity A; you support charity B. You have no time for A; I regard B as a bunch of dubious characters who ought to have been stripped of their charitable status years ago. The advantage of the present system is that I support the charity I like and you support the charity you like. If I were compelled to support B and you to support A, the financial flows would be the same; but the economic gain would diminish or disappear. This is the economic advantage of voluntary dispositions over constrained transfers such as taxation.

Temporary or permanent saving?

Saving is *temporary* if it is made and realised for a particular purpose such as a holiday or a pension. Saving is *permanent* (or *perpetual* or *in perpetuity*) if it is never drawn down.

It is sometimes argued that the only rational motive for saving is increased consumption. But the opposite idea, that saving can or should be in perpetuity, is clearly expressed in the Old Testament, although economic terminology is not used.[4]

Saving in perpetuity is a retrospective rather than a prospective concept. At the time of the original saving the saver may have no intentions as between temporary saving and saving in perpetuity. Permanent saving becomes part of the capital stock like any other saving; it is identified as permanent retrospectively, by virtue of never being drawn down.

The desire to bequeath, by contrast, is a prospective rather than a retrospective concept. The desire to bequeath need not imply a desire to save in perpetuity. The testator may bequeath capital for consumption, although for bequests to individuals this is seldom the explicit intention and the results of its realisation are bizarre: in particular, a family that had built up capital during the first generation would run it down during the second, for no obvious reason and in contravention of the widespread notion that each generation is and should be more prosperous than its predecessor. Within the trust sector, the testator intentionally restricts the freedom of the beneficiaries to dispose of the assets in trust; outside the trust sector, the assets are under the control of the beneficiaries, to keep or to spend: but even here, it is generally common ground between testator and beneficiaries that (taxation

---

4   The rationale of saving in perpetuity is discussed in Annex A to Chapter 4.

permitting) the assets should be built up rather than drawn down.

Is it possible to save up for death duties? This depends on the rate of tax. Kaldor has shown that, as the rate of tax rises, saving up for death duties is, first, possible and not irrational, second, possible but pointless and, third, impossible.[5] I have shown that it is irrational for the testator to absorb the tax fully, however low the rate at which it is levied.[6] But what is the likelihood that the testator will seek to absorb the tax at all? That is the subject of the next section.

Target or maximum?

Most taxes have both a price effect (the taxed good or service becomes relatively more expensive) and an income effect (the taxpayer becomes poorer as a result of the tax). If the price effect outweighs the income effect, disbursements on the good or service fall; if the income effect predominates, net-of-tax disbursements still fall,[7] but gross-of-tax disbursements rise. This is true of expenditure, earning, saving/investment, giving/bequest.[8]

---

5   Nicholas Kaldor, 'The Income Burden of Capital Taxes', *Review of Economic Studies*, summer 1942. This article by Kaldor is criticised in Appendix vii C (iii) of my *The Measurement of Fiscal Policy: An Analysis of Tax Systems in Terms of the Political Distinction between 'Right' and 'Left'*, Confederation of British Industry, 1971; now obtainable from the author. This critique is integrated into my *The Wealth of Giving: Every One in His Inheritance*, op. cit., pp. 41–2, 47, 61–2, 64–5, 79–84, 100–8.

6   *The Wealth of Giving*, op. cit., pp. 47, 80–1.

7   With the minor exception of Giffen goods, explained later.

8   All these activities concern two parties, two active parties for expenditure, earning and investment and one active and one passive party for giving and bequest. Taxes on all four activities fall on both parties, except at the logical extreme where one party absorbs the taxes entirely. All four taxes may be regarded as taxes on the payer if the tax on earnings is treated as a tax on the employer (which is how it is collected) rather than on the employee.

Thus a tax on earnings results in higher gross-of-tax earnings if the income effect predominates. This happens either at low levels of income (where there is little margin for survival) or if the taxpayer is aiming at a particular standard of living (a target) rather than seeking to make his standard of living as high as possible (a maximum). The concept of a target is equally valid for saving: when repayment of tax on pension fund income was discontinued in 1998, for example, taxpayers were warned that they would have to save more in order to enjoy any given target income as pensioners.

The concept of a target is in principle equally valid for giving and bequest; and the consequences of a tax-induced rise in gross-of-tax giving and bequest are fully analysed in *The Wealth of Giving*.[9] The question arises, however, whether such targeting is of any importance in practice. Why would anyone increase his gross-of-tax bequests when death duties rose and reduce them when death duties fell? In particular, why should anyone wish his heirs to have a particular standard of living and ownership, so that he would make up any shortfall and pocket any surplus? The idea is so bizarre that it is hard to conceive of anyone behaving like that; it is an economist's Empty Box, a conceptual possibility that remains permanently uninhabited. The testator is more likely to bequeath more when bequest is cheaper and less when it is dearer and leave adjustment of lifestyles to changing tax rates to be effected by the next generation along with many other adjustments unforeseeable at the time of bequest.

The testator is much more likely to be a maximiser than a targeteer, maximising bequest along with other goods and services in

---

9   See note 5 on p. 34.

a pattern of disbursements determined by his preferences (and price elasticities) and by the tax-inclusive prices of bequest and its competitors. In the course of much reading and listening on the subject of death duties, I have yet to hear of a testator or a potential testator who was a targeteer rather than a maximiser. Targeteers are unknown to tax advisers and the taxpayers they advise. They are the ghosts in the Empty Boxes of authors sympathetic to death duties.

Rationalism and irrationalism

So far, the argument has assumed that the economic agent, the taxpayer, the testator, is economically rational. But is this so? Or should it be so? And what if it is not?

Judicious economists and those with a background in other subjects have always recognised that economics is only part of life and not necessarily the most important part. *Homo economicus* is a logical and unattractive extreme.

In the Lionel Robbins Memorial Lectures *Rationality, Utility and the Mind*, given at the London School of Economics in March 1998, Professor Daniel Kahneman applied this insight to the terrain of economics itself. In a series of examples, he showed how economic behaviour itself might be modified by non-economic considerations. For example, why do so many people leave a tip in a restaurant that they have no intention of ever revisiting? This behaviour may be economically irrational; but it is not irrational. They leave tips because doing so is in their sight normal or expected or accepted or fair. These explanations are rational, although they are hardly economic.

This monograph assumes that the testator is economically rational. This is important because much of the argument is not easy to substantiate empirically. In this monograph, the testator may make mistakes (as all economic agents do); his behaviour may be rational but not economically rational in the manner explained by Kahneman; but he is not economically irrational in any sense that threatens the argument of the monograph.

Forms of death duty

A substantial proportion of economic and other literature on death duties is concerned with their form. Should they be levied on the testator/donor or on the recipient/donee? Should spouses be exempt? Should children or other blood relations enjoy preferential treatment? Should intestacy attract a heavier rate of duty, as in the proposal of Bentham?[10] Or, in the high-flown social engineering of Rignano,[11] should the 'same' money attract higher and higher rates of duty with each inter-generational transfer?

Some forms of death duty, actual or proposed, like interspousal exemption, amount to a reduction in the burden and as such are welcome; others, like the social engineering of Rignano, amount to an increase and are unwelcome. The reintroduction of a charge to capital gains tax on the occasion of death could be worse than most forms of death duty. But forms of death duty are not discussed here. In a range of typical situations, such as the inheritance of a whole estate by an only child, the result may be similar or identical whatever the form. But more importantly, the

10   *Supply without Burthen, or Escheat vice Taxation*, J. Debrett, 1795.
11   Eugenio Rignano, *Un Socialismo in Accordo colla Dottrina Economica Liberale.* J. Stamp, *The Social Significance of the Death Duties* (Noel Douglas, 1926) is adapted from the translation of Rignano by Dr Schultz.

question of the form of death duties is secondary to the question of their existence, just as the rival merits of hanging, shooting, poisoning, electrocuting and other possibilities may constitute a less than enthralling topic for those whose attitude to capital punishment is abolitionist.

In purchase and sale, both economic agents are active. In bequest and donation, the recipient is passive;[12] only the testator or donor is active. That is why it is beside the point to argue that the recipient does not deserve the money or money's worth that he receives. Many people do not deserve their good fortune; nobody deserves the public infrastructure of roads, schools, hospitals and other institutions which he inherits by virtue of being born. Any testator who wishes to disinherit an heir on grounds of demerit or otherwise is free to do so. But the merits or demerits of the heirs are of little relevance in logic or in practice. The testator/donor is the active party. It is he who decides the distribution of his assets between spending, investment, charitable giving, personal giving and other uses – ultimately between spending and bequest. It is his actions which are affected and his incentives which are impaired by death duties, even if they are levied on the recipient.

To put the same point differently, the possibility of bequest is one of the reasons for making money and one of the reasons for saving money. For the entrepreneur with his millions and the small saver with his thousands, the effect of death duties is the same, a discouragement to the making of money and an encouragement to spending it rather than saving it once it is made.

---

12   Apart from his contribution to the two *echo effects* explained in *The Wealth of Giving*, op. cit., pp. 87–8.

Palliative or cure?

The discussion of palliatives follows on from the discussion of forms of death duty. Reliefs may make a bad tax less bad. Business and agricultural property relief effectively exempt qualifying business and agricultural property and resolve the problem for the taxpayers concerned. Other reliefs are less effective. In particular, conditional reliefs for privately owned country houses and their lands and the National Trust regime for the estates in their hands are mitigations, not solutions. For those who manage to stay out of the hands of the National Trust, death duties still add to the already heavy burden of keeping the estate going. Those who find surrender to the National Trust the least unattractive option see the family ownership that gave the estate its life and character replaced by institutional and bureaucratic control – preferable perhaps to ownership by the state, but institutional and bureaucratic none the less.

The palliative of reliefs is no substitute for the cure of abolition.

Lessons from abroad

This monograph argues the case for abolishing death duties in a British context. Although most of the arguments are equally valid for other countries, there is no need for a comparison between British death duties and death duties elsewhere. But two lessons from abroad are worth noting.

First, over the last generation, Australia, Canada and New Zealand have abolished death duties, principally in response to tax competition. These are all countries with close links with and similarities to the United Kingdom. As far as I know, abolition has had no adverse consequences, politically or economically. I attended a tax congress in Sydney in 1978, when abolition was new and topical, and asked as many Australians as I could whether it had caused any problems; none said yes. In the United States, the case for abolition is being argued with increasing frequency and conviction; abolition is on the political agenda.

Second, the European Commission has in recent years taken an increasing interest in intergenerational transfers of businesses.[13] The Communication of 31 December 1994 says: 'The Commission requests the Member States to reduce the burden of taxation on the transfer of businesses effected in the form of *inter vivos* gifts, or transmission on death (inheritance tax, gift tax, registration fees), as in the British system, with the aim of ensuring that this taxation policy is better adapted to ensuring the survival of businesses ... The British "Business Relief" scheme consists of total tax exemption on business transfers applicable to the assets of an enterprise as long as the heirs continue the activities of the enterprise for a certain time.' Thus the Commission itself recommends the British system of exemption (or abolition of the tax) for business assets. The Groupement Européen des Entreprises Familiales, an association of family companies in a number of European Union member states, is seeking to make exemption of business assets general throughout the EU.

The case for exempting business and agricultural assets is

---

13 'Communication from the Commission on the transfer of business. Actions in favour of SMEs' (small and medium-sized enterprises), *Official Journal of the European Communities* 94/C 204/01, 23 July 1994; 'Communication on the Commission recommendation of 7 December 1994 on the transfer of small and medium-sized enterprises', *Official Journal* 94/C 400/01, 31 December 1994; 'Communication from the Commission on the transfer of small and medium-sized enterprises', *Official Journal* 98/C 93/02, 28 March 1998.

stronger and more palpable than the case for exempting assets in general; but the arguments are structurally similar, and a widespread regime of exemption for business assets must weaken the rationale for death duties on assets of other kinds.

Simplicity and complexity

Arguments for and against death duties operate in a number of interrelated dimensions, some complex and technical. The present monograph has mentioned, rather than discussed, a number of these dimensions, focusing instead on the political and economic heartland of the subject – economic taxable capacity, saving in perpetuity, the capital dimension of prosperity, the relative prices of saving and spending, equality. The summary treatment of the topics merely mentioned in the present chapter makes it possible to abbreviate and simplify the presentation of the whole.

Within the heartland of the subject, some arguments are straightforward while others are technical. I have tried to provide a single document useful both to those who are professionally equipped to cope with the technicalities and to those who are not. For the former, the footnotes and annexes provide proofs and other supplementary material that technicians have a right to expect. For the latter, the text is intended to be intelligible independently, although all footnotes and annexes are mentioned in the text and can be followed up where the reader considers this useful.

I have resisted the temptation to reproduce proofs and supporting arguments from *The Wealth of Giving* and other previous publications. The general reader may well not wish to have technical proofs, and the specialist can find them in the sources cited.

The bibliography is in two parts. The first contains the works cited elsewhere in the monograph. The second mentions other works of note on death duties. Until about a generation ago, most publications on death duties argued in their favour; more recently, the majority have been against.

How important are death duties?

For several thousand years, death duties, where levied, were generally an impediment rather than a killer,[14] a cost imposed by government on necessary transactions, perhaps comparable with the present British stamp duty on house purchase. It was only in the nineteenth century, under the influence of the French Revolution, totalitarianism and social engineering, that death duties were conscripted into the task of remoulding society and levied or advocated at confiscatory rates. In 1949, estate duty on estates of £1 million and above was raised to 80 per cent. Since then the rate has become proportional, not graduated, at 40 per cent on estates exceeding £242,000 (in 2001/02); but £242,000 is less than the price of a family home in much of the South-East and elsewhere. Death duties are heavy where they fall; and they have the notable quality (by contrast with income tax, in particular) of falling predominantly on middle wealth, since under any tax regime there will be more scope for avoidance by the rich, through emigration or otherwise.

---

14 'Killer' was the description of death duties used by the National Association of Manufacturers, a trade association consisting predominantly of small firms which was one of the three bodies that amalgamated into the Confederation of British Industry (CBI) in 1965. I salute the NAM here for being far-sighted and for being right. A generation or more later, even the CBI, the British government and the European Commission can no longer deny the truth of what the NAM was saying in the 1960s and earlier.

Death duties are often a neglected topic because they affect only a minority of taxpayers each year, a minority selected by the hazards of mortality. But those affected are hit hard at 40 per cent: their families are prevented by taxation from doing what most families take for granted, increasing in prosperity from generation to generation. The changing social background to death duties is discussed in Chapter 8. Death duties have few committed advocates nowadays; their principal ally is inertia. That is why the topic is important: death duties should not be allowed to rest in peace.

3 ECONOMIC TAXABLE CAPACITY

The concept of *taxable capacity* or *ability to pay* is important both in the theory of public finance and in the politics of taxation. The taxpayer should be taxed according to his ability to pay. The trouble with this idea is that it is vacuous. It purports to mean something while really meaning nothing.

There are two senses of *ability to pay*. The first is formal, a truism. The taxpayer has taxable capacity as long as the tax collector can collect the tax. He has taxable capacity right down to his last crust. In the same sense a slave or a prisoner is able to work as long as he does not collapse. All this says nothing about the best way of treating taxpayers or prisoners.

The second sense of *ability to pay* purports to be substantial. The rich should pay more tax than the poor because they have more taxable capacity. Yes, but how much more should they pay? And how is this taxable capacity measured? The only answer is a long silence.

This traditional concept of taxable capacity addresses single taxpayers, whether individual or corporate. It compares them with each other one by one. The only useful conclusions to emerge from these comparisons are, first, that taxpayers in like situations should be treated alike (the criterion of *horizontal equity*, in so far as *like situations* can be identified) and, second, that poorer taxpayers should not be taxed more heavily than richer. I call this the criterion of *vertical inequity*; as we see later, it is frequently violated by death duties. The criterion of *vertical equity* (that rich taxpayers should be taxed more heavily than poor) is vacuous, because it gives no indication of how much more heavily the rich should be taxed and is compatible with anything from proportional taxation to total confiscation of everything exceeding the average.

The effects of a tax can be more usefully assessed by a criterion that addresses them, not *individually* (how the tax affects one taxpayer relatively to another), but *socially* (how the tax affects taxpayers in aggregate). This task is performed by the criterion of *economic taxable capacity*.[1]

Any successful act of tax collection takes a sum from the taxpayer and transfers it to the fisc.[2] In addition, there are the costs of collection, which fall on the fisc, and the costs of compliance, which fall on the taxpayer. Collection costs have a monetary value explicitly and compliance costs have a monetary value implicitly.[3]

---

1 Barry Bracewell-Milnes, *The Taxation of Industry: Fiscal Barriers to the Creation of Wealth*, Panopticum Press, London, 1981, pp. 51–3; Barry Bracewell-Milnes, *The Wealth of Giving: Every One in His Inheritance*, op. cit., p. 83.

2 In corrupt systems, what reaches the coffers of the fisc is less than what leaves the pocket of the taxpayer. Under a system of tax farming, the tax collector is remunerated by keeping for himself a proportion of the tax he has collected. Even if the proportion is precisely defined, this system gives both the tax collector and the Treasury an incentive to be extortionate. Tax collectors (called *publicans* in the King James Bible) were unpopular in the New Testament because they had an interest in increasing the tax take. The same would be true in the United Kingdom if there were substance in the accusations made from time to time that tax officials are promoted according to how much tax they have taken and not merely how efficiently they have applied the law. I am abstracting from all these refinements here.

3 'Though vexation is not, strictly speaking, expense, it is certainly equivalent to the expense at which every man would be willing to redeem himself from it' (Adam Smith, *The Wealth of Nations*, v, ii, ii). Smith's vivid term *vexation* means the same as the more neutral modern phrase *compliance costs*.

The sum of collection costs and compliance costs is sometimes called administrative costs. I am not discussing compliance costs further here, although they can be very high for inheritance tax, perhaps higher than for any other form of taxation, not least because compliance costs may be substantial even where the tax liability eventually proves to be zero.[4]

Even if administrative costs were zero, taxation still imposes costs on the economy and society additional to those represented by the tax itself. These are the costs of *economic distortion* or the *tax wedge*, the costs of dislocating the price relationships of a taxless world. At present, the United Kingdom government is taking some 40 per cent of gross domestic product (GDP) and 45 per cent or more, nearly half, of national income. If taxation takes half of national income, on average it doubles the cost of everything. For example, the white-economy firm that pays employer's and employees' national insurance contributions, pay-as-you-earn income tax and value-added tax may have a cost structure about twice as high as a black-economy firm, which is not obliged to carry the burden of government on its back. The doubling of costs does not leave taxpayers' behaviour unaffected. Some respond by operating in the black economy, some by emigrating, some by abandoning projects or operations that would have been financially self-supporting in a taxless world. Tax distortion or the tax wedge is the increase in costs caused by taxation. The taxpayer's response is either evasion (like cigarette smuggling) or avoidance (like cutting down smoking). Only at the logical extreme is the taxpayer's behaviour unaffected by a large tax-price differential.

---

4 When my mother died in 1993, it took me three weeks' full-time work to establish that there was no liability to inheritance tax. This experience is normal.

The concept of *economic taxable capacity* compares the amount of tax collected with the amount of economic disruption caused by the process of collection. *Economic taxable capacity* is the excess of the yield of a tax over the social loss it inflicts. This social loss excludes the yield of the tax and thus assumes, however optimistically, that the social benefit from government expenditure equals or exceeds the taxpayer's loss. Thus, a tax base has economic taxable capacity of 20 if the yield is 100, the administrative costs are 30 and the costs of dislocation are 50:

$$20 = 100 - 30 - 50$$

In what follows, administrative costs are ignored, although it frequently happens that these costs are a large or even an infinite multiple of the tax yield.[5] The argument is always strengthened if administrative costs are included; but without them we have a simplified relationship:

$$\pm A = B - C$$

where A is economic taxable capacity, positive or negative; B is the yield of the tax; C is the cost of the economic dislocation caused by the tax. C includes the amounts of other taxes lost to the Revenue as a result of the economic dislocation. For example, if the level of the primary tax (say, value-added tax or inheritance tax) makes it impossible for a firm to continue in business, the fisc loses what that firm would otherwise have paid in secondary taxes such as employer's and employees' national insurance contributions, pay-

---

5   As in the example of my mother's liability to inheritance tax, note 4 above.

as-you-earn income tax, corporation tax, value-added tax, excise duties ... The secondary losses of the fisc alone may be a large multiple of the primary gain; and the losses of the rest of the economy are additional and may be much larger.[6]

Examples of tax bases with negative economic taxable capacity include income subject to tax at rates in excess of the maximum revenue rate. For example, if the rate of income tax that maximises the revenue yield is 50 per cent gross, then the yield is reduced by increases in the rate above this level and increased by reductions towards 50 per cent. Evidence from the United Kingdom and the United States shows that reductions in very high rates of income tax have increased both the amount of tax and the proportion of total tax contributed by richer taxpayers.

It is sometimes argued or assumed that taxes are mere transfers and that what is lost by one party (the taxpayer) is gained by another (the fisc). This is wrong for taxes in general (as I have argued above) and for death duties in particular. The critical distinction is between voluntary transfers which are wealth-creating and involuntary transfers which are wealth-destroying. Financial gain or loss must be distinguished from economic gain or loss. Paying £1,000 to your son or a charity may be financially the same as paying £1,000 to your tax collector; but it is not the same economically. The first two are voluntary; the third is not. Voluntary giving and bequest are not mere neutral transfers but a source of wealth creation: giving is economically preferable for the taxpayer, more

---

6 There are also third-round effects, often favourable to the fisc, as when the labour and capital released by the failure of firms in the second round find alternative employment. However, even if the labour and capital are fully re-employed, the pattern of activity is still distorted, and the value of production reduced, by the effects of taxation.

attractive, more wealth-creating than any alternative use of his funds.[7]

I have shown elsewhere[8]:

(i)   that a tax on giving always causes a social loss;
(ii) that the social loss (or wealth destroyed) always at least equals the revenue yield;
(iii) that the social loss always exceeds the revenue yield if gross-of-tax giving decreases in response to the tax;
(iv) that the social loss exceeds the revenue yield even if gross-of-tax giving remains constant or rises, except in the limiting case.

Thus, except in the limiting case, giving and inheritance have negative economic taxable capacity: the damage the taxes do exceeds the revenue they yield. $C > B$ in the algebra on p. 47 and A is negative. This refutes argument (1) at the end of the Introduction.[9]

---

7   *The Wealth of Giving*, op. cit., passim.

8   The mathematical proofs of these proportions are given in *The Wealth of Giving*, op. cit., pp. 79ff. In *the limiting case*, the curve of donor's surplus is parallel to the 45° line of tax neutrality. *Donor's surplus* is the excess of the utility of a gift to an effective altruist over the market value of the asset concerned. Donor's counter-value is the utility of the gift to the donor that just matches his financial loss. The limiting case is mentioned for the sake of completeness; but it is of little or no practical importance.

9   The additional wealth created by personal giving, although fully appropriated to personal use, is a *public good*, in the technical sense of a good or service the use or enjoyment of which by one person does not reduce the amount available for use or enjoyment by others. *The Wealth of Giving*, op. cit., p. 61.

4   SAVING IN PERPETUITY

Every frugal man is a public benefactor

ADAM SMITH[1]

This chapter is about perpetual saving, or saving in perpetuity. Perpetual saving is not to be confused with repeated saving, annual saving or contractual saving – additional saving in each year of the saver's life. Perpetual saving may represent a single act of saving or a succession of acts. It is saving that is never drawn down, whatever the reason and whether or not it was planned as perpetual saving from the outset.

The concept of perpetual saving has been ignored, misrepresented or belittled by mainstream economic writers; but it is a biblical concept (even though it is not a biblical expression) as well as being a commonsense secular idea, widely understood and accepted today, as it has been for thousands of years. Perpetual saving is linked to giving, inheritance and bequest, since the individual saver is not immortal.

Saving and consumption

Saving initially depresses consumption, although it may increase

---

1   *The Wealth of Nations*, Book ii.

it subsequently. A subsequent increase in consumption is some-times said to be the only rational purpose of saving; but this is not so: perpetual saving is sometimes a preferable use of funds and no less rational than consumption.

Consumption and saving may be represented respectively as the actual and potential use of resources; perpetual saving is then a potential use that is never realised. *Use* in this sense is not identi-cal to *enjoyment.*

Annex A to this chapter explains the rationale of perpetual sav-ing. Money saved may be worth more to an individual in any year than the same money spent; and this relationship may continue year after year until his death.[2]

The technical argument of Annex A is confirmed by common sense. Mises speaks of 'prolonging the period of provision beyond the actor's own life'.[3] Alfred Marshall's assertion[4] that parents wish to leave money to their children is corroborated by daily ex-perience. In the 1990s it was becoming a matter of increasing po-litical concern that rising longevity and the cost of savers' nursing care in their final years were absorbing resources that both testa-tors and legatees wished to retain as legacies. The idea of wealth cascading down the generations was used as a political slogan.

If the one-generational model of atomistic individualism

---

2   Annex A is taken from pp. 20-5 of *Land and Heritage: The Public Interest in Per-sonal Ownership*, Hobart Paper 93, IEA, London, 1982. I have also discussed sav-ing in perpetuity in the following: *Is Capital Taxation Fair? The Tradition and the Truth*, Institute of Directors, London, 1974, pp. 40, 61–7 (where the concept of perpetual saving is discussed, though not so called); 'A Liberal Tax Policy', *British Tax Review*, 1976, pp.115–17; *The Taxation of Industry*, op. cit., pp. 51–3; *The Wealth of Giving*, op. cit., p. 85.

3   *Human Action*, William Hodge, London, 1949, p. 496.

4   *Principles of Economics*, Macmillan, London, 1961, Book iv, Chapter vii, para. 6.

were a good representation of the real world, people would invest their money in annuities that terminated on their death. In fact, apart from pensions, where such investment is compulsory, only a minority of assets are so invested. Heritable assets are preferred.

The saver or frugal man is a public benefactor, particularly if his saving is in perpetuity. Because the perpetual saver prefers the shadow of potential use to the substance of actual use, the rest of society enjoys a permanent loan at rates chargeable for loans with maturity dates. The temporary saver is a producer, the perpetual saver a producer-consumer. It is because the act of saving is for him its own reward that the saver in perpetuity confers such a benefit on the rest of society.

The realisation of the wealth available from perpetual saving requires that the assets concerned be owned by a single owner or a small number of owners with a strong sense of common identity (husband and wife, a religious house ...). State ownership of assets destroys the wealth otherwise available from perpetual saving through the process of *dilution*: the individual's interest in state-owned assets is too diluted to be of any significance, economically or otherwise, or of any benefit to himself or others.

Use and enjoyment

The enjoyment of a good or service is often realised through its use. A house, a car, a suit of clothes, a compact disc may be enjoyed by virtue of being used. But there is more to enjoyment than this. The legal term *enjoyment* includes potential use as well as actual. A holiday home is enjoyed in this sense even when it is not occupied;

a car is enjoyed even when it is not being driven. They are available, at the owner's disposal.

Thus, the *first difference* between use and enjoyment is that use is actual, whereas enjoyment includes potential use. It is rather like a multi-stage game of chance. You have won in the first round, and you have qualified for further play in the second round without increasing your stake. Your win in the first round is like the actual use of your holiday home. Your qualifying stake in the second round is like its potential use. The qualifying stake is worth something, it is better to have it than not to have it, it may have a market value and be saleable; this value increases if you make winning throws but disappears if you make losing throws. Similarly, the value of potential visits to your holiday home increases if they are realised and disappears if they are not.

The *second difference* between use and enjoyment does not depend on the realisation of potential. If you neither visit nor let nor lend your holiday home for a whole year, this need not imply that the value you have had from it is zero (or negative after the payment of expenses). Potential use is not just a qualifying ticket for the second round which becomes valueless if you make losing throws. For many, if not for all, potential use has its own value, is its own kind of realisation.

In the simplest and clearest illustration, trading and market value are absent. Caged animals do not play with their toys all the time; but they grieve all the time if their toys are taken away. Conversely, the pleasure given or the value created by the toys can be independent of their use. Similar examples might be given for children or other humans who are not financially self-supporting.

When adults are managing their own assets, these truths may be obscured. Financial motives may be assumed to explain everything (which will be true only in the limiting case): for example, it may be assumed that the owner who makes little use of his holiday home is seeking a capital gain. But, even if he is seeking a capital gain, this may be only a partial explanation of his behaviour. And if he neither seeks, expects nor realises a capital gain and yet incurs significant expenses for the upkeep of a property he hardly uses, the simplest explanation is that he derives value from the enjoyment of his property additional to the value derived from its use. Perpetual saving is by definition an example of this second difference between use and enjoyment, this second excess of enjoyment over use.

For many activities and situations, use and enjoyment are co-terminous, complementary and different names for the same thing. In other activities and situations, covering *inter alia* saving in perpetuity and giving, the relationship is reversed; use and enjoyment are competitive: the less the use, the more the enjoyment.

Use and potential use are in competition with each other, whether in ordinary life or in a city under siege: if you eat your store of food, if you drink your cellar dry, you lose both their future use and the ability to look forward to their future use. The more the use, the less the potential use. This is also true of activities and situations, like perpetual saving, in which use is permanently forgone. The more the use, the less the potential use. The difference is that in ordinary living use and enjoyment are complementary: the more the use, the more the enjoyment. Under perpetual saving, use and enjoyment are competitive: the less the use, the more the enjoyment. This distinction is missed both by traditional economics and by much religious and other social comment: perpetual saving means perpetual abstinence; the higher the level of perpetual saving and the personal wealth that it implies, the less the spending of the rich and the more the resources that are available to the rest of society.[5, 6]

The *third excess* of enjoyment over use is altruistic in origin and thus has a logic diametrically opposed to that of welfare economics and relative poverty. It is the enjoyment an individual derives from objects that he neither uses nor owns and which may be owned by someone else or may not be owned by anyone. Most members of the Royal Society for the Protection of Birds are not ornithologists or bird-watchers. Most members of the Historic Churches Preservation Trust will not visit more than a tiny proportion of the churches whose fabric their subscriptions serve to maintain. Most people who would like to arrest the destruction of rainforests are not seeking to visit them or exploit them economically. It is possible to derive more, not less, enjoyment from your neighbour's estate if you know that it is left in peace, instead of being infested with ramblers. A particularly poignant example is provided by Antarctica. There are those who regard any human contact with the last wilderness as a form of violation. This is not irrational, although others will differ. Those who share this opinion derive pleasure not from owning, visiting or exploiting Antarctica, but from its being left in peace.[7]

---

5   In its simplest form, the argument assumes that Say's Law holds good, that supply creates its own demand, and that resources are fully employed. Even if this were not so, through excessive taxation, for example, or government regulation, death duties are never imposed as a remedy for underconsumption or excessive saving, nor would they be effective for this purpose.

6   The argument applies to assets in general; but it applies with particular force to large country houses and the like, whose personal owner is performing an easily identifiable public service. *Land and Heritage*, op. cit., pp. 80–6.

7   For these people, Antarctica has *existence value*, a recent coinage denoting the value created by the knowledge of the existence of something which itself has value.

There are many situations in which it may be rational (and normal or usual) for an individual to rejoice in the existence or deplore the destruction of things or works which he will never enjoy as owner or user. It is not irrational to regret the destruction of the lost books of Livy without having read the books that remain. It is not irrational to deplore the cultural genocide in Tibet without being a Buddhist or a Tibetan or knowing Tibetan or having any intention of visiting Tibet.

Although *existence value* is a powerful influence and motive for many people, saving in perpetuity has an additional element of value through ownership.

Given the mortality of human agents, saving in perpetuity implies giving or bequest. Bequest also requires an element of saving in perpetuity, since a bequest normally represents saving otherwise than for consumption by the testator. If the amount bequeathed is constant or rises over time, savers collectively are saving in perpetuity as well as for consumption, any drawing down of savings by one group of savers being compensated or overcompensated through an increase in perpetual saving by others.

Incentives

A tax on income from work has a price effect (it makes work more expensive by comparison with leisure) and an income effect (it reduces income by comparison with the tax-free situation). If the taxpayer's principal motive is survival, the income effect predominates at the bottom of the scale, and an income tax gives the taxpayer an incentive to work harder. As the taxpayer becomes more prosperous, the price effect becomes increasingly important relatively to the income effect, and the income tax gives the taxpayer

Diagram 1　**Taxpayer response to a tax on work**

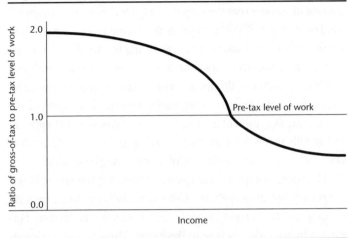

an incentive to work less and to take more leisure instead of pay devalued by taxation.

In Diagram 1, the horizontal scale shows pre-tax income and the vertical scale shows the response of taxpayers to a flat tax of 50 per cent gross. (Gross-of-tax income 100, tax 50, net-of-tax income 50.) The response can be that of a single taxpayer in different situations or that of taxpayers in aggregate. Initially, gross-of-tax income almost doubles as the taxpayer tries to maintain his income. This effect weakens as income increases. Gross-of-tax income falls to the level of pre-tax income and below, although the ratio never falls to zero.[8]

The relationship is similar for temporary saving such as saving

---

8　Since the curve never falls to zero, it must have a point of inflexion, which is put in Diagram 1 at the level of pre-tax income.

for a pension, although here the determining variable is the amount of income that the taxpayer requires his savings to generate. For example, if the taxpayer is determined to have a pension worth half his final salary, a tax on saving (or a reduction in the yield from saving) will impel him to save more. As salary and pension income increase, this income effect becomes less important by comparison with the price effect, the higher cost of saving relatively to spending as a result of the tax. The ratio of gross-of-tax to pre-tax saving falls to the level of pre-tax saving and below, although it never falls to zero unless the rate of tax on saving is prohibitive.

The relationships are completely different if the saving is not temporary but in perpetuity. There is no income effect, because the taxpayer is not trying to maintain or achieve a particular standard of living, either now or in the future. There is only a price effect. Saving in perpetuity is a form of luxury good or service in the technical sense of a good or service with a high income elasticity of demand.[9] Goods and services with a high income elasticity of demand generally have a high price elasticity of demand; so the volume of saving in perpetuity can be expected to be substantially reduced by taxation.[10]

---

9   Saving in perpetuity is by definition *not* a luxury good or service with the popular connotation of high living and high spending, since saving in perpetuity precludes the high spending with which it competes.

10 Saving in perpetuity is not an example of the two categories of goods or services, the demand for which rises instead of falling in response to a rise in price. The first category is the fashionable goods discussed by Duesenberry and others which are bought because they are expensive. If the taxpayer were interested in following fashion like this, he would not be forgoing such purchases by saving in perpetuity. The second category is Giffen goods (named after the inventor of the concept, Sir Robert Giffen), of which the only important example is staple foods of the poor (bread in England): the substitution effect is outweighed by the income effect of a price change.

This refutes argument (2) at the end of the Introduction. The economic agent, the active party, is the testator; the legatee is passive. Death duties make saving in perpetuity more expensive for the testator and must be expected to reduce the volume of such saving and the benefits it confers on society.

5 THE CAPITAL DIMENSION
   OF PROSPERITY

In a socialist economy there are capital goods, but no capital. The notion of capital makes sense only in the market economy.

LUDWIG VON MISES[1]

The notion of perpetual saving and the wealth it creates, like the notion of capital, makes sense only in a market economy. Wealth can be created by perpetual saving only under personal ownership. Under state ownership, although perpetual saving is possible, nobody enjoys the wealth it creates – only (at best) the income it generates.

Perpetual saving is part of the capital dimension of prosperity. It is often assumed or implied that economic prosperity is unequivocal, that if an individual is more prosperous than others in one way he will be more prosperous in other ways and more prosperous in general. With minor exceptions and qualifications,[2] this belief is incorrect: as this chapter shows, it is common, even normal, for one individual to be more prosperous than another in one

---

1   *Human Action*, op. cit., p. 264.

2   In particular, although invalid in general, the idea that economic prosperity is one-dimensional is valid at the extremes. If A has investment income that supports spending at a higher level than B's total income from labour, and B's earnings are rising no faster than A's spending, A is unequivocally more prosperous than B.

way but less prosperous in another way, and there may be no valid concept of prosperity in general.

Chapter 4, above, shows that the theory and practice of saving in perpetuity imply a preference for potential over actual use of assets. Assets can be enjoyed without being used; and this enjoyment is as much a component of economic prosperity as enjoyment on income account, enjoyment through use.

Prosperity is thus not one-dimensional (a function of the standard of living) but at least two-dimensional (a function of prosperity on income account and prosperity on capital account).[3, 4]

The importance of the capital dimension of prosperity varies with the level of income. It is of negligible importance below a certain minimum; it becomes more and more important as income rises, since spending rises more and more slowly. The capital dimension will thus become more and more important as a result of economic growth.

Annex A discusses the two forms of prosperity. If economy or individual A has wealth of 100 and income of 2 and B has wealth of 50 and income of 4, it is not possible to say unequivocally that either is more prosperous than the other. If the ratios of income to capital are market-led and reflect productivities and preferences in the two economies, each economy is at the point that best suits its own particularities. But, if the capital dimension is ignored and the aim of policy is merely to maximise income, it is possible to identify

---

3   Capital values corresponding to the gross domestic product have for some years now been produced and published by the Central Statistical Office.

4   The relationship between capital and spending is both complementary and competitive. For given levels of yield the relationship is complementary: the more the capital, the more the spending. For changing levels of wealth the relationship is competitive: spending is reduced by new saving and increased by the drawing down of old saving.

and quantify the damage done by moving a capital-intensive low-yield economy away from its most favoured position.

Professional opinion on this subject is confused. A buoyant stock market is generally (and rightly) perceived as a sign of economic prosperity, although it is (rightly) recognised that a boom may go too far, as happened to the Japanese stock market in the 1980s. But for house prices a different climate of opinion prevails: rising house prices are a form of 'asset price inflation' and are thus as undesirable as rising prices of food, clothing or consumer goods. And there is often a puritanical dislike of what are seen as unearned increases in wealth, even if this additional prosperity is widespread.

I have taken issue with this line of argument elsewhere.[5] Rising house prices have more in common with rising share prices, and indeed with rising prices of rare stamps, than they have with rising prices of food, clothing and consumer goods. All must retain a link with reality if they are to avoid doing more harm than good: for house prices the main link is the earnings of owners and potential owners, for shares it is income yield and for stamps it is actual or potential interest rates (the opportunity cost of holding). As long as these and perhaps other indicators are not emitting danger signals, an increase in asset prices means an increase in prosperity. The householder is right to feel more prosperous as his house becomes more valuable.

Subject to the constraints of prudence, prosperity is increased by rising asset prices. But the second dimension of prosperity, wealth, creates conflicts, not between rich and poor or capital and labour or producers and consumers, but between old savers and new savers. Old savers[6] gain from a combination of rising income

---

5 'In Praise of Rising House Prices', *Economic Affairs*, Dec. 1988/Jan. 1989.

and falling yields leading to still more rapidly rising asset values. For new savers, the main or only consideration is a high yield at the time of asset purchase. As soon as the asset is purchased, the new saver becomes an old saver for that asset and is interested in rising income, falling yield and still more rapidly rising prices. Many or most savers are new and old savers at different times for different assets and have their own conflicts of interest between these different capacities. Since houses, shares and stamps are durables and food and clothing are not, there is no comparable conflict of interest between new and old consumers of food and clothing. With minor qualifications, consumers share the same interest, which is low and falling prices. Old savers have the opposite interest, which is high and rising prices. That is why the concept of inflation is inappropriate to assets and the concept of 'asset price inflation' is misleading.

Simons right and Simons wrong

Savings are expenditure.

HENRY SIMONS[7]

WAR IS PEACE
FREEDOM IS SLAVERY
IGNORANCE IS STRENGTH

GEORGE ORWELL[8]

Annex A to Chapter 4 discusses the rationale of perpetual saving

---

6   Unless their money is on deposit with a bank or building society, in which case their interests are the same as those of new savers.

7   *Personal Income Taxation*, University of Chicago Press, Chicago, 1938, p. 97.

8   *Nineteen Eighty-four*, Martin Secker and Warburg, London, 1949, Part i.

and cites the remark of Henry Simons that 'many people save instead of consuming'. Annex B to the present chapter addresses in more detail the distinction between saving for use and saving in perpetuity. Saving for use is part of the production process and may in that capacity offer a base for taxation. The saver in perpetuity, by contrast, has a dual role as producer and consumer and in that capacity confers large benefits on the rest of society. But saving in perpetuity offers no usable tax base: the damage done by distortion of the saver's behaviour always exceeds the yield of tax,[9] and the destruction of the benefits otherwise available to the rest of society is additional.

In Annex A to the present chapter the overall prosperity of the inhabitants depends on subjective discount rates and other elements of personal preference. At one extreme, if wealth is held in perpetuity as a means of generating an income in perpetuity, the value of the parent capital may be of little or no importance,[10] unless tax is levied on this value, in which case a capital gain that appears to increase prosperity really has the opposite effect.[11] At the other extreme, someone who has exhausted the possibilities of additional spending may still be interested in increasing his wealth: for increases in prosperity, the capital dimension is important to him, the current account is not.

Simons was writing with a tax perspective.[12] His purpose was

9   This assumes that perpetual saving, as a luxury good, has a more-than-unitary price elasticity of demand (is relatively price elastic). The amount saved (in the sense of savings *turnover* or *disbursements* on saving) therefore falls faster than tax revenue rises as the rate of tax increases.

10   I have discussed this scenario in *The Taxation of Industry*, op. cit., Appendix i.

11   This *farmers' paradox* is discussed in *Land and Heritage*, op. cit., pp. 11, 44.

12   He confesses: 'thus tardily that our remarks about the definition of income have been coloured not a little by considerations of tax policy' (*Personal Income Taxation*, op. cit., p. 100).

to establish the rationale of comprehensive income taxation, including earned income, investment income and realised capital gains on the income side and consumption and new saving on the outgo side. He sought to tax all the disparate components of the total similarly and to this end exaggerated the similarities between them and minimised the differences. Hence the Orwellian pre-echo that *savings are expenditure*.

The present monograph, by contrast, seeks to elucidate the differences between these disparate components and to examine the implications of these differences for tax policy. In particular, the capital account is an important component of prosperity; but it offers little if any scope for taxation without the infliction of disproportionate damage. The present monograph likewise distinguishes between temporary saving (which is part of the production process and may have a limited potential as a tax base) and saving in perpetuity (which is not part of the production process and cannot be taxed without the infliction of disproportionate damage). Simons noticed that 'many people save instead of consuming',[13] and this at least he got right. But he misinterpreted his own insight. The choice between saving and consuming is not of the same order as the choice between smoking pipes and smoking cigarettes, as Simons held; the choice between saving and consuming has a moral dimension, and the two have very different economic consequences. Still less is it right to assimilate disparates to each other as a preliminary to taxing them similarly. The individual has a choice between spending, saving, giving, lending, hoarding and other possibilities. If his judgment is not distorted by taxation, he will make the choice that offers the best

---

13   *Personal Income Taxation*, op. cit., p. 95.

outcome, the largest accretion of wealth and/or worth. The task of public policy is so to shape the tax system as to impede this process of value creation as little as possible. In particular, policy should seek to distinguish money flows and stocks with potential as tax bases from flows and stocks with no such potential. Simons, with his impulsion to assimilate the unassimilable, is working in the opposite direction.

Conclusion and implications for policy

The capital equivalent of prosperity on current account is eroded or destroyed under socialism and fellow-travelling creeds, through the complementary forces of dilution and barriers to trade.

Ownership *dilution* (or dispersal or dissipation) is the destruction of value (or the prevention of its realisation) through the reduction of ownership *intensity*. Dilution can add to losses caused by costs of trade, barriers to trade and institutional inadequacy. Even under a market system, a small holding of shares may be worth little in the capital dimension because the costs of sale would absorb most of the proceeds. And dilution intensifies the defects of a socialist or communal system. For example, if a small number of people have communal rights to the use of a piece of land, they may be able to agree arrangements to reduce inefficiency of use (the tragedy of the commons); but this becomes more and more difficult as their numbers rise.

Barriers to trade may destroy value in the capital dimension either through explicit government restrictions and regulations (like the United Kingdom restrictions on the beneficiaries' use of private-sector pension funds) or through the lack of institutions enabling the capital dimension to be enjoyed through trading (like the lack of access to the capital dimension of State Retirement Pensions). Collectivist expropriation of privately owned assets does damage not only in the income dimension (because the assets are less efficiently used) but also in the capital dimension: they cannot be freely bought and sold (or bought and sold at all), and the economic value of ownership is destroyed because the assets are not owned by anyone. Socialism can destroy the economic value of private ownership under capitalism; but it cannot provide a socialist alternative, since no such alternative exists. The full realisation of capital values requires not only private ownership but also a transparent and articulate system of property rights so that rights can be exchanged between willing buyers and sellers until they come to rest with the owner who values them most highly.[14]

The lesson for public policy is that the capital dimension of prosperity should be nurtured and cultivated, not neglected, damaged or destroyed. Government policies affecting prosperity on current account generally or always have a corresponding potential for affecting prosperity on capital account. Prosperity on capital account is eroded or destroyed by capital taxation, expropriation and other forms of government regulation and intrusion; it is realised through personal ownership, articulated property rights and a comprehensive and efficient capital market.

---

14 For debts, the argument is reversed: opacity (the lack of transparency) is an advantage. A major reason why in a prosperous and well-run economy the National Debt should be positive, not zero, and should generally increase from year to year, is that collective debt is not perceived as a burden like private debt.

6 THE RELATIVE PRICES OF SAVING AND SPENDING

The ultimate destination of all taxpayers' funds is either saving or spending. What is not saved is spent and what is not spent is saved. Both giving and minor categories of disbursement like lending, hoarding and gambling may be classified ultimately as spending or saving or a mixture of the two.

Taxes on saving are cumulative, whether levied on the yield or on the parent capital. The cumulative total may be computed as a proportion of the capital or as a proportion of the yield.[1]

Since the value of savings is what they will buy, and this value is reduced by taxes on spending, a tax system is neutral between saving and spending when all taxes on saving are zero.[2]

Taxation affects the prices of spending and saving and thus their prices relatively to each other. Under the definition of neutrality in the previous paragraph, a tax system is neutral if tax is levied on spending at a positive rate (such as 25 per cent net[3]) and saving is not taxed at all. Any tax on saving makes the saving of taxpayers liable to the tax more expensive by comparison with spending and thus their spending cheaper by comparison with saving.

---

1   *The Measurement of Fiscal Policy*, op. cit., Chapter vii B, Appendix vii C.
2   ibid., Chapter vii B.
3   A net tax is levied on a base excluding the tax, like value-added tax; 25 is levied on a tax-exclusive base of 100. A gross tax is levied on a base including the tax, like income tax; 20 is levied on a tax-inclusive base of 100: − 25 per cent net = 20 per cent gross: 25/125 = 20/100.

In the United Kingdom, inheritance tax and other death duties have always been levied on a well-to-do minority. Inheritance tax makes the rich man's saving more expensive and thus cheapens his spending. At a gross tax rate of 40 per cent, he can have 100 of spending for an opportunity cost of 60 of saving, the other 40 being paid for by the Treasury in lost inheritance tax. His spending is also cheapened relatively to the spending and saving of the poor man or non-inheritance-tax-payer; 100 of spending costs the poor man an opportunity cost of 100 of saving and 100 of saving costs him 100 of spending. The rich man has 167 (= 100 ÷ 0.6) of spending for 100 of his own saving or for 100 of the poor man's spending or saving. Inheritance tax reduces the cost of the spending of the rich relatively to their own saving and to the spending and saving of the poor. The tax privilege enjoyed by the spending of the rich increases as the other taxes on saving are brought into the reckoning.[4]

The social engineering or fiscal engineering of inheritance tax is thus in precise opposition to an earlier form of fiscal engineering: *sumptuary taxation.* There the idea was to impose additional taxation on items of expenditure that characterised the lifestyle of the rich: a coach and eight, for example, might attract a heavier tax than a coach and four on the argument that a man who could afford the extra four horses could afford the heavier taxation. The concept of sumptuary taxation lingers on in the value-added tax, which commonly distinguishes between more and less necessary goods and services and taxes the more necessary less heavily or not at all. Although I am no enthusiast for sumptuary taxation (preferring a more neutral system), I recognise that it has the merit of a

---

4   'The Hidden Costs of Inheritance Taxation', op. cit., viii 2.

certain populist logic and popular appeal. I can find no merit, economic, social, moral, egalitarian or otherwise, in an anti-sumptuary tax like inheritance tax, which grants tax privileges to the spending of the rich relatively to their own saving and to the saving and spending of the poor.

Spending and saving in perpetuity are jointly exhaustive and mutually exclusive logical categories for the financial dispositions of individuals. Everything that is not spent is saved and everything that is not saved is spent. There is no escape from the logical dilemma that rich people cannot at the same time be overtaxed relatively to poor people both on their spending and on their saving: it is a fiscal Position Impossible. If they are overtaxed on one, they are undertaxed on the other. Inheritance tax overtaxes the rich taxpayer's saving and thus undertaxes his spending. In a consistent system (thus one not subject to retrospective additional charges on savings accumulated under a more favourable or less hostile regime), the taxpayer's choice between spending and saving is respected; and this implies a zero rate of inheritance tax.

This refutes argument (3) at the end of the Introduction. Wealth is capitalised saving and does not constitute a separate tax base. Inheritance tax has the perverse effect of making spending cheaper for the rich than for the poor.

The argument of this chapter is not lost on the taxpayers concerned, who frequently increase their spending towards the end of their lives in order to avoid death duties. Inheritance tax not only cheapens the opportunity cost of spending by the rich; its perverse pricing also leads to perverse redistributive results. That is the subject of the next chapter.

7 EQUALITY AND DEATH DUTIES

For the classical liberal it is a contingent fact that there is no universal consensus on what a just or fair income distribution should be.
Egalitarianism is therefore to be rejected as the norm for deriving principles of public policy.

DEEPAK LAL AND H. MYINT[1]

The principal argument for death duties over the last century or so has in practice been the argument relating to equality: death duties increase equality and reduce inequality. This argument is the subject of the present chapter.

Equality in the twentieth-century sense is the combination of envy upwards and altruism downwards. This combination has no biblical authority and is specifically condemned by St Basil;[2] its elevation to the status of an ethical ideal with claims on the attention of Christians is in a historical perspective a post-Christian heresy.

Equality in this twentieth-century sense is also a recent innovation; the word was used in different senses until the end of the

---

1   *The Political Economy of Poverty, Equity and Growth*, Clarendon Press, Oxford, 1996, p. 38.
2   'It is senseless for men both to hate their superiors and to love their inferiors', *Letters*, cxv.

nineteenth century and beyond.[3] The present chapter contrasts the earlier meanings with the modern meaning; notes the ambiguities in the modern meaning; and analyses the internal contradictions of attempts to reduce the inequalities of both spending and saving.

Within the tradition of economic thought, there has been a conflict between those who accept equality as an ethical ideal and those who do not. There has also been a separate but related conflict between those who regard a significant loss of economic output as an acceptable price to pay for a reduction of inequality and those who do not.[4] The present chapter, by contrast, argues that egalitarianism is by its own standards self-contradictory (since a reduction in the inequality of spending implies an increase in the inequality of wealth) and that a tax-induced reduction in the inequality of spending increases instead of reducing the amount of economic output.

Meanings

The best guide for policy is the principle that income taxes should diminish systematically an objectively measurable kind of inequality.

The criterion of equity, by itself, leads only to a vague and elusive ideal, not to a sound and workable income tax.

There is always a danger in a practice of compromising . . .

---

3   *Égalité*, part of the threefold inspiration for the French Reign of Terror in the early 1790s, was a perverse variant of these earlier senses; it had nothing to do with the twentieth-century sense of statistically measured identity of economic outcome.

4   Henry Simons makes his preference clear: see the quotation on p. 79, below.

> *between the requirement that taxation shall mitigate an objective*
> *sort of inequality and the requirement that relative levies on*
> *individuals shall find approval in some sense of reasonableness.*
> *Sentiments of fairness cannot be ignored; but ... income taxes*
> *should diminish the inequality of income, letting the chips fall*
> *where they may.*

HENRY SIMONS[5]

Annex A to this chapter compares earlier meanings of *equality* with the twentieth-century statistical meanings. The earlier meanings are human in scale: they concern dealings with known or identifiable individuals. The terms mentioned include fair and honest dealing, giving each man what is due to him by nature, distribution according to worth, impartiality, absence of privilege, reciprocal self-help, justice and fair dealing, proportionality, horizontal equity, equal dignity, equal power, equal ability or achievement, fairness, equity, equability.

By contrast, statistical equality is totalitarian in the sense of totalitarian envy. Just as strangers can be made enemies by war between nations, so within a nation stranger can be set against stranger and class against class by totalitarian envy and statistical equality. Everyone is conscripted into the class war. Conscientious objection is not permitted. No one is remote enough to escape.

Simons expresses his preference for statistical over human-scale equality without compromise. The best guide for policy is that income taxes should diminish inequality. Equity leads only to a vague and elusive ideal. Compromise poses the danger that taxes on individuals will find approval in some sense of reasonableness.

---

5   *Personal Income Taxation*, op. cit., pp. 138, 139, 31.

Sentiments of fairness notwithstanding, income taxes should diminish the inequality of income, letting the chips fall where they may. This last appeal to the ethics of the gaming house is particularly telling: by his own account, Simons is using the armed force of the state to gamble with other people's money. Whereas human-scale senses of equality create value through the voluntary principle, taxation is as voluntary as burglary.

So what are 'an objectively measurable kind of inequality' or 'an objective sort of inequality', whose diminution or mitigation takes priority over equity, sentiments of fairness and a sense of reasonableness? How is inequality to be measured? Short of complete equality,[6] how can an acceptable degree of inequality be identified? And what reduction in inequality can justify what sacrifice of equity, sentiments of fairness and a sense of reasonableness? If Simons knows the answers to these questions, he does not share them with his readers. On the evidence of his most influential and mischievous book, Simons is entirely innocent of statistical understanding. In this he resembles the vast majority of egalitarian sympathisers in politics, the churches and elsewhere.[7]

Belief in equality is thus a superstition in the precise sense of a

---

6 'Every increase in the degree of progression is, *with reference merely to distributional effects*, a desirable change, and without limit short of substantial equality among those taxed' (p. 17; emphasis in original). By *degree of progression*, Simons means a graduation of income tax rates such that taxpayers higher up the scale pay tax at higher or much higher rates than those lower down. Simons does not attempt to define or measure the degree of progression, perhaps believing it to be a commonsense concept, which it is not. The degree of progression is a concept no less complex and ambiguous than the related concept of the degree of inequality. The measurement of progression is discussed in my *The Measurement of Fiscal Policy*, op. cit.

7 Although a small minority are statistically numerate or even professional statisticians. For the majority, *where ignorance is bliss, 'Tis folly to be wise.*

tenet, scruple or habit founded on fear[8] or ignorance. But there the resemblance ends; and the comparison is not flattering to egalitarianism. The worship of Moloch may have been cruel and mistaken; but it was not irrational in the sense of being internally inconsistent. We now turn to the ambiguities and self-contradictions of equality.

Ambiguities

There is a basic ambiguity about the equalitarian objectives of a graduated tax.

A graduated tax necessarily involves the comparison of more than two classes.

WALTER BLUM AND HARRY KALVEN[9]

During the whole range of life of commercial society, from the end of the Middle Ages to our day, the wealth of the rich merchant has been resented far more than the pomp of rulers.

(BARON) BERTRAND DE JOUVENEL[10]

This section, which summarises Annex B, moves on from the different meanings or senses of equality to the varying interpretations of these meanings. There is no single concept of equality or

---

8 'Mitigation of the grosser inequalities in the distribution of income, wealth and power would surely fortify the existing system against attack and contribute to the prospects of its stability and security. Thus, highly progressive taxation might serve, historically, to sustain and strengthen the incentive to accumulation'. *Personal Income Taxation*, op. cit., p. 22.

9 *The Uneasy Case for Progressive Taxation*, University of Chicago Press, Chicago, 1953, p. 97.

10 *The Ethics of Redistribution*, Cambridge University Press, Cambridge, 1951, p. 79.

inequality, and the neglect of these differences of meaning and interpretation leads to the contradictions of policy and practice discussed under the heading 'The over-determination of policy', below.

By way of example, if a woman is promoted and breaks through a glass ceiling that previously reserved senior positions in her profession for men, her move increases equality between the sexes but reduces the equality of women and may well reduce economic equality overall (because the share of a highly paid group has risen). Many of the people who support equality between the sexes also support economic equality and are unaware of the inconsistency between the two.

Absolute equality may be unattainable, even if it were desirable, between even small groups of separate persons, since their very separateness carries connotations of inequality. This is illustrated by the difficulties of interpreting the Christian doctrine of equality.

Christians believe that they are equal before God (who 'is no respecter of persons', Acts x, 34). 'They which shall be accounted worthy to obtain that world, and the resurrection from the dead . . . are equal unto the angels; and are the children of God, being the children of the resurrection' (Luke xx, 35–6). But at once there are difficulties. St Paul says: 'I am the least of the apostles, that am not meet to be called an apostle, because I persecuted the church of God.' (I Corinthians xv, 9). Differences between Christians were later formalised by the process of sanctification.

A system of equality before the law is preferable to one in which justice is bought and sold or enforced sporadically. But attempts to realise this concept are fraught with difficulty. How can there be equality between an individual citizen and a government department funded by the bottomless purse of the taxpayer? How, and at what cost, is it possible to eradicate the prejudices of judges and juries against certain categories of defendants and in favour of others? Where illegal immigrants, asylum seekers and political refugees are concerned, what does equality before the law mean when the matter in dispute is whether they are entitled to its protection?

'The dimensions of equality' in Annex B discusses ten forms of economic inequality which are variously inconsistent with each other in the manner explained above for the feminist's glass ceiling.

'The measures of inequality' in Annex B addresses the question of how inequality is to be measured when the identity of the variable (such as net-of-tax income) and the statistical basis of the computation (the amount of net income for each member of the population) are not in dispute. It notes that there is an infinite variety of measures of inequality (in other words, there is no limit to the number of different ways in which inequality can be measured). The section goes on to consider whether and how far a distribution that is more unequal than another by one measure of inequality may be less unequal by another measure. The section concludes that there is no upper limit to this process of reversal. In other words, however large the difference, two statistical measures of inequality can always be found such that a distribution is more unequal than another by one measure and less unequal by the other.

Among the many possible measures of inequality, Annex B opts for the SUMDC (simple unit mean deviation coefficient), which is the easiest to understand and compute, is not totalitarian and thus ignores intra-sectoral transfers that do not affect the main distinction between the shares of richer and poorer citizens.

77

Thus the ambiguities of the concept of equality or inequality extend from the field of its operation to the method of its measurement. No one coefficient can be expected to reveal the whole truth about the dispersion of a distribution of many members or even as few as three members, each of which may vary independently of all the others. Moreover, the concept of equality itself has serious deficiencies as a political ideal, because in many of its senses it has no close connection with serious policy aims like the reduction of poverty, and it may even operate in the opposite direction.

Even more important is the opposition between economic and political inequality. In a situation where the state takes and spends about half the national income and interests itself in almost every aspect of the citizens' lives, economic inequality, however large, serves to provide a counterweight to the over-mighty powers of politicians and bureaucrats and a focus of resistance to elective dictatorship.

Vertical inequity

Beyond the ambiguities considered in the last section are anomalies in the sense of internal policy inconsistencies and contradictions. Death duties, like capital gains tax, are a fertile breeding ground for *vertical inequities*, situations in which the richer taxpayer pays less tax and the poorer taxpayer pays more. The reason for these anomalies is that the logical framework for vertical equity is comparisons within a year; death duties and capital gains tax, by contrast, have a timescale that can extend over a generation or more, during which richer and poorer taxpayers may alter their relative positions or change places.

In 'Lifetime Cumulation of Transfers'[11] I addressed the vertical inequities caused by levying death duties (then called capital transfer tax) cumulatively on the taxpayer's transfers over life and on death. Four causes of vertical inequity under lifetime cumulation are inflation, economic growth, variations in yield and political changes. Other anomalies are that lifetime cumulation reduces tax revenue and that lifetime cumulation may make the tax system less 'progressive'.[12] Lifetime cumulation of transfers was reduced to ten-year cumulation in 1981 and seven-year cumulation on the introduction of inheritance tax in 1986.[13]

The over-determination of policy

Prevailing opinion to the contrary notwithstanding, it is only an inadequate degree of progression which has no effect upon production and economic progress.

HENRY SIMONS[14]

I propose to skirt this field of combat and shall assume here that redistribution, however far it may be carried, exerts no disincentive influence, and leaves the volume and growth of production entirely unaffected.

(BARON) BERTRAND DE JOUVENEL[15]

---

11   *British Tax Review*, June 1979.

12   ibid., p. 372.

13   Seven vertical inequities inherent in capital gains tax are discussed in Section 8 ('Inequity between taxpayers') of my 'Capital Gains Tax: Reform through Abolition', in *A Discredited Tax: The Capital Gains Tax Problem and its Solution*, Readings 38, IEA, London, 1992. Death duties and capital gains tax constitute the inner sanctum of vertical inequity.

14   *Personal Income Taxation*, op. cit., p. 19.

15   *The Ethics of Redistribution*, op. cit., p. 3.

The ambiguities and incompatibilities inherent in the concept of totalitarian equality and its measurement lead to policy over-determination. Over-determination is the specification of more in-dependent policy objectives than the logic of the subject permits, the addition of further objectives when the degrees of freedom are already exhausted. It is like a set of equations with more equations than variables: unless the redundant equations merely repeat in-formation already available, the resulting solutions are contradic-tory. The ten concepts or dimensions of inequality in Annex B, for example, do not offer independent choices or policy objectives: they have implications for each other.

Chapter VII of *The Measurement of Fiscal Policy* identifies the three principal measures of fiscal policy as the height of the tax sys-tem, the basis of the system (the relative taxation of saving and spending) and the intension of the system (the relative taxation of rich and poor).[16] These three are independent of each other: each can be varied independently of the other two. But together they ex-haust the degrees of freedom. Thus, it is possible to tax the rich at the same rates as the poor or more heavily, and it is possible to tax saving at the same rates as spending or more or less heavily, and it is possible to tax rich savers more heavily than poor savers – or rich spenders more heavily than poor spenders; but it is not possi-ble to make both the spending and the saving of the rich more ex-pensive[17] than those of the poor (for example, through a graduated – or 'progressive' – expenditure tax and graduated death duties). The reason is that spending and saving are jointly exhaustive and

---

16   There are also secondary measures: p. 71 and Appendix vii.

17   More expensive by reason of taxation. For example, some 80 per cent of the retail price of petrol is taxation: tax makes petrol five times as expensive as it would be otherwise.

mutually exclusive categories: everything that is not spent is saved and everything that is not saved is spent. Spending and saving have a rate of exchange against each other, like the pound and the dollar. A graduated expenditure tax that makes the spending of the rich more costly than that of the poor necessarily makes their saving cheaper; graduated death duties that make the saving of the rich more costly than that of the poor necessarily make their spending cheaper. This is seldom, if ever, the purpose of graduated death duties; but it is their result. Similarly, a lower inequality of wealth leads sooner or later to a higher inequality of spending.[18] This is explained in Annex C.[19]

Once it is recognised that equality and inequality are not one-dimensional concepts but multidimensional, the traditional structure of the argument breaks down or goes into reverse. The traditional starting point is alluded to by Simons. Equality is alleged to be a good but in conflict with prosperity. There must be a trade-off between the two goods, the terms of trade being determined by the opinions of the traders (that is, those taking the political decisions that affect the outcome). In this scenario, classical liberals and free marketeers will accept only a small or very small reduction in prosperity as the price of an increase in equality; Simons will accept 'a distinctly adverse effect upon the size of the national income'. The next stage in the argument is the contribution of de Jouvenel. 'The special merit of de Jouvenel's treatment is that he completely waives any objections to the levelling of incomes

---

18   In *Redistribution in Reverse* (Aims of Industry, 1974), I showed that more equal shares of wealth mean less equal shares of spending. The argument is developed further in Annex C to this chapter.

19   Annex C is based on my paper 'The Hidden Costs of Inheritance Taxation', op. cit.

resting on incentive grounds and proceeds to consider the issue solely in ethical terms.'[20] While I accept de Jouvenel's contention that the case against redistributive taxation need not be argued in terms of incentives or material prosperity, I maintain that the reduction or abolition of redistributive taxation can benefit both rich and poor in terms of both equality and prosperity. This is explained in Annex D.

The traditional concept of the trade-off between equality and prosperity is represented by the cake and the slice. If redistributive taxes are reduced and incentives are improved, the size of the cake will increase. The poor will have a smaller share of a larger cake, and they may gain more from the increase in the cake than they lose from the reduction in their share; even if they do not gain absolutely in this way, the increase in the size of the cake means that there is more to distribute, so that prosperity increases on average and overall. This argument may have its uses; but it is not the one I am advancing here.

The new elements introduced into the cake-and-slice argument by Annex D are saving in perpetuity (which is enjoyed simultaneously by owner and user) and the distinction between the inequality of spending and the inequality of wealth. If output is unaffected by taxation (incentive effects are zero), the effect of increased taxes on saving in perpetuity is to reduce the proportion of output spent by the poor (expenditure plus the use of saving in perpetuity) and increase the proportion of output spent by the rich. There is no trade-off between equality and output because output is unaffected and taxation aimed at the rich merely increases the inequality of spending. If output rises when taxes fall,

---

20 Blum and Kalven, *The Uneasy Case for Progressive Taxation*, Preface, p. vi.

there is again no trade-off between equality and output: the reduction of taxes on saving in perpetuity increases output and reduces the inequality of expenditure and may reduce inequality overall.

Saving in perpetuity is important in this monograph because it is a form of costless wealth creation, benefiting owner and user simultaneously; and the reduction of taxes on saving in perpetuity, by benefiting rich savers, reduces the inequality of spending and may reduce inequality overall. Finally, saving in perpetuity is economically significant because it is not subject to the law of diminishing marginal utility.[21]

Conclusion

Stuff'd guts make no musick: strain them strong and you shall have sweet melody.

CHRISTOPHER SMART[22]

Equality has many meanings and is beset with ambiguities. The confusion is at its worst in the area of economic or totalitarian equality, the twentieth century's contribution to turning civil society into a Hobbesian war of all against all.

As an ethical ideal, equality has the remarkable property of being desirable only in limited quantities. There are few advocates of complete equality enforced by the state: such a polity would make Stalin's Russia or Pol Pot's Cambodia seem benign. Most

---

21 The law of diminishing marginal utility, on which modern economics rests, states that a given individual at a given time derives less and less benefit (or utility) from the use of successive units of any good or service or from spending in total. It can be generalised to cover lifetime spending and temporary saving, but not saving in perpetuity.

22 *Jubilate Agno* xi, 12.

egalitarians therefore settle for limited equality or a degree of inequality. *Hinc illae lacrimae*: this is where the trouble starts.

The first problem is that most limited egalitarians are not capable of identifying the best position even in their own terms. Simons speaks of a 'degree of inequality' and a 'degree of progression';[23] but *degree* in this sense is not a social rank or an academic award, it is a statistical measure: and yet he gives no hint of how this measure is to be computed. Unless Simons knew more than he divulged, it follows that he had no means of identifying 'the optimum degree of progression'[24] and would not have recognised it if he had met it in the street.[25]

The second problem for limited egalitarians is that of incommensurability. Total equality under government coercion is generally unacceptable because it would involve totalitarian terror and the reduction or even annihilation of measured economic output.[26] That is why they settle for limited equality. I have argued in the preceding paragraph that limited egalitarians who are not statisticians have no means of computing degrees of progression, let alone identifying 'the optimum degree of progression' (if such a

---

23 *Personal Income Taxation*, op. cit., p. 19.

24 ibid.

25 The 'degree of progression' can be computed in various ways; I proposed my own measure (intension) in *The Measurement of Fiscal Policy*, op. cit. Like equality/inequality, and for similar reasons, progression (or progressivity) is a statistical measure that is not answerable to common sense alone. Moreover, progression contains an internal contradiction to which there is no analogue in inequality. The most widespread notion of an increase in progressivity is an increase in the steepness of the curve of graduated tax rates as it rises to a given maximum (the curve moves to the left towards the origin and reaches the maximum sooner); but I have shown in *The Measurement of Fiscal Policy* (p. 9) that the limit of this process is a strictly proportional tax with progressivity of zero.

26 Subsistence, household and barter activities, which are not components of gross national product, would survive and indeed thrive.

phrase is susceptible of construction). But this is not the worst. If equality is a good, the attainment of which is constricted by conflicting aims such as the containment of totalitarian terror and the prevention of collapse into a subsistence economy, what are the trade-offs and who decides what? How much loss of output is acceptable to achieve an increase in equality which most limited egalitarians would not be able to quantify? What are the trade-offs between equality and terror? This is not a remote question for taxpayers who have been subject to dawn raids and other variants of what Adam Smith called 'the frequent visits and the odious examinations of the tax-gatherers'.[27] And the taxpayer with right on his side can often not afford to pursue his case against the tax authorities because they are supported by public funds (and thus by moneys contributed under compulsion by taxpayers including the frustrated litigant). The incommensurability of equality and the constraints on its realisation are not like the incommensurability of the square and the circle or even the welfare of one individual and the welfare of another; if an ethical ideal can be realised only by unacceptable means, these necessary accoutrements raise fundamental questions about both the ideal and its ethics.

Worse is to come. The traditional framework of debate has been between equality and prosperity, both seen as goods. The more of one, the less of the other: the terms of trade varying with ideological proclivities, classical liberals favouring prosperity and socialists favouring equality.[28] De Jouvenel was perhaps the first to

---

27   *The Wealth of Nations*, Book v, ii, ii.
28   'The transition to a fiscal system in which every tax would have some substantial justification would appear, therefore, to require increasing the contribution of the personal income tax many fold' (*Personal Income Taxation*, op. cit., p. 40). Whether 'many fold' means three times, four times or more, Simons makes clear the implications of egalitarian redistribution.

move away from this dispute and discuss (and attack) the ethics of redistribution on their own terms. While I accept de Jouvenel's argument, I go farther and maintain that the pursuit of equality through taxes with an effective incidence on saving in perpetuity increases the inequality of spending and may increase inequality overall. It also reduces the prosperity of poor as well as rich; but I keep this argument in reserve, in order not to revive the argument about prosperity versus equality, which de Jouvenel waived. The arguments against egalitarian taxation are strong enough on ethical and indeed egalitarian grounds; arguments relating to prosperity are merely a welcome bonus. My innovation is to argue against egalitarian taxation on the chosen ground of the egalitarians: the taxation of saving in perpetuity will increase the inequality of spending and may increase inequality overall.

Saving in perpetuity is important because ultimately whatever is not spent is saved. Simons was right to identify the phenomenon of saving in perpetuity; but his policy implications were perverse.

'Stuff'd guts make no musick,' says the poet: 'strain them strong and you shall have sweet melody.' The central argument against egalitarianism is that it is self-contradictory and perverse on its own terms and its own chosen terrain of debate. This is due to over-determination and other forms of logical confusion in a subject that cries aloud for tautness and precision. The loss of prosperity, not least for the poorest members of society, is additional. The unnecessary expansion of the state sector of the economy, with its inevitable inefficiencies, adds a further dimension of loss.[29]

---

29 'The alternative, technocratic approach to poverty alleviation is by contrast necessarily infected with egalitarianism because of its lineage ... Given the ubiquitous assumption of diminishing marginal utility underlying the approach, any

This chapter refutes (4) at the end of the Introduction.

normative utility weighting of the incomes of different persons or households leads naturally to some form of egalitarianism. But this smuggling in of an ethical norm which is by no means universally accepted leads to a form of "mathematical politics" ... This is a thin edge of a very big wedge. Besides leading to recommendations for all sorts of redistributive schemes, it also leads to a vast increase in *dirigisme*. To alleviate poverty, an end embraced by classical liberals, on this route they are being led to endorse the creation of a vast Transfer State, which in the long run could be inimical to the growth and poverty-redressing effectiveness of a market economy.' Lal and Myint, *The Political Economy of Poverty, Equity and Growth*, op. cit., p. 39. The 'ubiquitous assumption of diminishing marginal utility' is rejected by the present monograph as inapplicable to saving in perpetuity. The latter, combined with the distinction between the inequality of wealth and the inequality of spending, destroys the egalitarian argument like a house of cards.

8   THE SOCIAL BACKGROUND

The rates of estate duty rose substantially during the 45 years between the introduction of the tax and the outbreak of World War II. They were further increased to sacrificial levels early in the war. For some 35 years after the war reductions in death duties were widely regarded as politically impossible. Arguments for lower rates of duty were not refuted or even answered but ignored. Indeed, there was talk of a wealth tax in the 1960s; and the death-duty regime was made more onerous when estate duty was replaced by capital transfer tax (with its lifetime cumulation of transfers[1]) in 1975.

Reductions in death duties over the last twenty years indicate a change in political perceptions. Lifetime cumulation of transfers was replaced by ten-year cumulation in 1981. The top rate of tax, which was 75 per cent (gross) under capital transfer tax, has been reduced to 40 per cent. The increase in business and agricultural property relief in the 1980s and early 1990s to 100 per cent (thus exempting business and agricultural property) has enjoyed cross-party support.

The change in political perceptions mirrored changes in public attitudes. These changes themselves reflect changes in social and economic circumstances which are likely to continue and even in-

---

1   See p. 78, above.

tensify. This chapter seeks to identify some of the background changes that could make the reduction or abolition of death duties acceptable and welcome far beyond the ranks of those influenced by arguments from economic principle.

Inversion of the pyramid

When estate duty was introduced in 1894, there was a division of 10 per cent/90 per cent or thereabouts between a rich minority and the majority of the British population. This division manifested itself in dress and other externals and was impossible to miss. The main division now is between the prosperous majority of 90 per cent or thereabouts and an underclass of welfare-dependents without work or savings of their own. The rich, especially those who are rich on old money at risk from death duties, have lifestyles similar, particularly in externals, to those of most other people.

Multiple capacities

In 1894 Marxist single-capacity class structure may have been an approximation to reality: most workers rented their accommodation and few had substantial savings. Now most people are both workers and capitalists and landowners: a large majority own their own homes and a small majority have significant savings of their own. Sir William Harcourt's slogan 'we are all socialists now'[2] no longer has the resonance it had.

---

2 Harcourt was the Chancellor of the Exchequer who brought in estate duty in 1894; but this remark was made during the passage of Lord Goschen's budget in 1888.

Price of housing

The threshold for the start of inheritance tax is £242,000 in 2001/02, a sum that will now buy only a modest family home in London, the South-East and elsewhere. A large and increasing proportion of the population are aware that their home or their savings or both are at risk from the present structure of inheritance tax.

Demographic changes

The increase in longevity over the twentieth century has profound financial implications of which most people are acutely aware. Older people have heavier medical and related expenses as well as the normal requirements of an income; and those past retirement age constitute a growing proportion of the population. Much the best solution of an otherwise intractable problem is that they should fund themselves from their own savings. But death duties are diametrically opposed to this practice, since the rational taxpayers' response to death duties is to run down savings over the last decade or two of their lives.

Same-sex unions

Inter-spousal transfers have been exempt from tax since capital transfer tax was introduced in 1975. This treatment is more favourable than under the former estate-duty regime and more favourable than the treatment in many other countries. It has been in force for a generation and would be politically difficult or very difficult to rescind. But what if homosexual pressure groups lobby for the introduction of same-sex unions in the United Kingdom?

Annex A, from an apparently sympathetic source, gives the position in eleven countries at the end of 2000. The pressure groups have so far had their way on everything in Britain, and they have made it clear that their agenda is far from fulfilled. But the extension of inter-spousal exemption to same-sex unions would be an unprecedented test of public tolerance. It could attract sharp criticism from cohabiting men and women and from low-profile same-sex partners who have no wish to get 'married'. Anomalies would abound. On the other hand, if the activities of the pressure groups caused inheritance tax to collapse in a gale of ridicule, they would on this occasion enjoy the support of a much wider constituency than usual.

The financial and economic arguments for the abolition of death duties have always been strong. The social arguments are now also strong and becoming stronger.

9 CONCLUSION

The traditional argument against death duties is that they are damaging to the economy as well as to the taxpayer; a number of examples are mentioned above (p. 24). These criticisms are correct and important, and I have addressed them elsewhere;[1] but they are not the subject of the present monograph. Such economic disadvantages cannot be demonstrated with Euclidean certainty; and, even if they could, they might be accepted or even welcomed, in an effusion of moral superiority, as a price worth paying for equality, equity or justice.[2]

Bertrand de Jouvenel takes the debate to a second stage in *The Ethics of Redistribution*,[3] which is concerned not merely with death duties but with government redistribution in general. De Jouvenel waives (although he does not dispute) all the arguments of economic efficiency and challenges redistribution entirely on ethical grounds. Aficionados of death duties can still retort, however, that their concept of ethics is more ethical than his. It derives from the conceit or fancy of relative poverty,[4] the notion that economic

---

1   For example, in *Will to Succeed*, op. cit.

2   See the quotation from Henry Simons on p. 79, above.

3   Op. cit.

4   As usual, Henry Simons is on the wrong side. 'There is real point, if not truth, in the suggestion that, within wide limits, the quality of human experience would be about the same at one income level as at another if the *relative* position of persons and classes remained unchanged. Poverty, want and privation are in large measure merely relative' (*Personal Income Taxation*, op. cit., p. 25; emphasis in original).

wellbeing depends on position rather than possession, so that what the rich lose is by definition a gain for the poor.[5] Since they wish to benefit the poor,[6] any damage done to the rich is by definition desirable and any damage done to the economy is acceptable or even welcome.

It would be flattering and misleading to describe all this as a process of reasoning. 'What the mind sets up the mind can pull down', as A. E. Housman remarks in another context;[7] 'and fancies based on false reasons can be overthrown by true reasons. But if true reasons could overthrow this fancy it would have been overthrown long before our time ... Its strength is that it has no reasons, only causes. Its root is not in the mind but in the soul; and it partakes the solidity of its indestructible foundations, the sloth and vanity of man.'

The present monograph seeks to take the debate one stage beyond de Jouvenel and into the citadel of egalitarian reasoning. The aims of reducing the inequality of wealth and reducing the inequality of spending are ultimately in conflict. Egalitarians must choose between them. Not all aficionados of death duties are sunk in intellectual sloth and moral vanity, and some suffer intellectual discomfort from known inconsistencies in their position. This gives their critics purchase on the subject. Death duties increase

---

5   The notion of relative poverty, the guiding principle of the welfare state and the poverty lobby, is thus even more destructive than the notion of a zero-sum game (in which the gains of one party match the losses of another within a given total). Under relative poverty, the gains of one party match the losses of another however much the total shrinks. A market economy, with voluntary exchanges between buyers and sellers, is far more beneficial than a zero-sum game, since both parties gain: the exchanges would not take place otherwise.

6   They ignore the problem of welfare dependency, the damage done by government handouts to the recipients themselves.

7   *The Editing of Juvenal*, Preface of 1905.

the inequality of externally observable lifestyles and increase the inequality of power between the majority of the population and a small minority of politicians and bureaucrats. Not all egalitarians welcome these developments. Some moderate egalitarians regret the loss of output caused by redistribution and expect an identifiable egalitarian benefit in return. It must come as a disappointment to find that the egalitarian payoff is negative, an increase in the inequality of spending and lifestyles. To lose in terms of efficiency may be regarded as a misfortune; to lose in terms of equality as well looks like carelessness, which is just what it is. Fiscal policy-makers are obtaining perverse results from measures whose internal logic and interrelationships they have not troubled themselves to understand. Three minutes' thought would suffice to find this out; but thought is irksome and three minutes is a long time.

Inheritance tax has no boundary with income tax or any other tax, so that its abolition would be simple; and its yield is negligible in the scheme of things and probably offset or more than offset by reductions in the yields of other taxes, so that its abolition would be cheap, costless or better than costless. The tax may appeal to atomistic individualists, self-centred souls without pride of ancestry or hope of posterity; but most people's outlook has a social dimension, and their scale of values finds space, not only for themselves, but also for their family and the rest of society. In this perspective, inheritance tax does immense economic damage and is perverse and counterproductive for its own ostensible purposes, egalitarian or otherwise. It should be put out of its misery.

Annexes

CHAPTER 4, ANNEX A

THE RATIONALE OF SAVING IN PERPETUITY

The power to consume

Suppose a man has a net-of-tax income of £100, of which he spends £90 and invests the remaining £10 in liquid assets with a net-of-tax yield of 10 per cent. His subjective rate of discount is less than the market rate and so his power to consume in the future is worth more to him now than £10 of immediate spending. In the second year, his income is £101; but saving is attractive to him for the same reason as before, and he spends £90 and saves £11. Similarly, in all subsequent years he spends £90 and saves the sum of the original £10 and the rising income from previous investment.

This is not an intertemporal shift in consumption. The man's consumption is lower in every year than it would be if he were saving nothing; there is no rate of discount, positive or negative, at which his consumption is increased. The power to consume is preferred to its exercise. The preference is not irrational or perverse; it is a matter of individual choice.

Intertemporal shifts in consumption are conveniently thought of as shifts within a single human lifetime, whereas the preference for the power to consume over its exercise suggests a time-horizon extending beyond a single generation. These are the simplest and most typical cases, though they are not the only possibilities.

In the example just given, spending remains permanently at

£90; the income elasticity of demand for consumption is zero. This logical extreme was assumed in order to simplify the argument. It can be relaxed without weakening the argument, though at the cost of making it more complex.

Suppose that new saving remains at £10 and that spending rises to absorb the increasing income from investments: £90, £91, £92 ... etc. After ten years the man's consumption attains the level at which it would have remained if he had saved nothing, and thereafter it exceeds this level. Eventually the missing consumption (£10 + £9 ... + £2 + £1) appears to be made good and more than made good. But this is true only at a zero or low rate of interest. It is not true at or anywhere near an interest rate of 10 per cent, at which level the present discounted value of consumption in every year would be increased by saving less and spending more.

The subjective rate of discount, which makes saving attractive to the saver, is below the market rate.[1] The attraction of the power to consume also implies that the discount rate is positive; if the discount rate is negative, the motive for saving is not the power to consume but survival. It follows from the argument in the preceding paragraph that there is a break-even or watershed positive rate of discount below which consumption may be regarded as the purpose of saving and above which it cannot. Thus the four rates of discount are, in descending order:

(i)   the market rate;
(ii) the saver's subjective rate;

---

1   This *economic rent* from saving is analogous to consumer's surplus from purchasing.

(iii) the break-even rate;
(iv) zero.

At the two logical extremes, the saver's subjective rate may co-incide with the market rate or with zero; if the subjective rate is zero, so is the break-even rate. In the normal situation where the subjective rate is below the market rate but above zero, the break-even rate is below the subjective rate if the power to consume is the motive for saving. The three bands between the four rates of discount represent:

(a) from market rate to saver's subjective rate, saver's economic rent;
(b) from saver's subjective rate to break-even rate, power to consume;
(c) from break-even rate to zero, additional consumption.

The break-even rate is not a purely subjective rate, although it depends on the saver's preferences. If saving is mainly for consumption, the break-even rate is at or near the saver's subjective rate; if it is mainly for the power to consume, the break-even rate is little above zero; and if it is in perpetuity, the break-even rate is zero. Over any finite period during which net saving is positive (that is, new saving exceeds spending out of old savings), the pattern of positive and negative saving from year to year determines the break-even rate of discount below which aggregate consumption is increased by saving and above which it is reduced. If net saving is nil over the period, the break-even rate and the saver's subjective rate coincide; as net saving increases, the break-even rate falls relatively to the saver's subjective rate. The longer the term of saving in any period, the larger the volume of net saving (since more saving is outstanding at the end of the period, even if it is intended for spending later). So, in any given period, there is a positive relationship between the term of saving and its motivation by the desire for spending power rather than actual spending. If the period is extended into the future without limit, the distinction between short- and long-term saving disappears and the only relevant distinction is between saving which is realised for consumption and saving which is not.

Wealth without consumption

Under the heading 'The power to consume' we have already noted the difficulty of explaining saving as an activity motivated exclusively by the desire for increased consumption. Some patterns of saving reduce consumption in every period; others increase it only at rates of discount far below the market rate, the saver's own subjective rate and the rate that would make intertemporal shifts of consumption attractive. The power to consume has a value additional to that of its exercise.

By an extension of the same argument, wealth can have utility even if the connection with consumption is so attenuated as to disappear entirely. Just as at one extreme wealth can have value solely by virtue of increasing consumption through shifts over time, so at the other it can have value directly and in its own right. The power to consume is intermediate between these extremes. It serves no purpose to describe these advantages of wealth as yielding psychic consumption; this metaphorical use of the word 'consumption' has nothing to do with its ordinary sense.[2]

2   These advantages of wealth have economic *value* (they yield psychic *utility* or

A difference of opinion

The consensus among economists has been that the purpose of saving and ownership is to increase consumption. Professor Murray Rothbard, for example, argues: 'Saving and consumption are not really symmetrical. All saving is directed toward enjoying more consumption in the future. Otherwise, there would be no point at all in saving ... No one wants capital goods for their own sake. They are only the embodiment of an increased consumption in the future ... There is nothing, after all, especially sacred about savings; they are simply the road to future consumption.'[3]

This position is fully consistent with the use of saving to achieve intertemporal shifts in consumption. It is partly consistent with the concept of wealth as spending power. But, as we have seen under 'The power to consume', if the value of the spending power depends on its exercise, the discount rate required to yield an increase in consumption may be so low as to bear no relation to the market rate the saver receives or to the subjective rate he requires. And if the saver reinvests all his additional investment income, his consumption falls in every period and there is no rate of discount, positive or negative, at which his aggregate consumption increases.

Henry Simons takes a different line: 'The observable fact is that many people save instead of consuming ... To assume that all economic behaviour is motivated by desire for consumption goods, present and future, is to introduce a teleology which is both useless and false ... In a world where capital accumulation

---

satisfaction); but it is confusing, and even the opposite of the truth, to describe them as yielding psychic *consumption*.

3   *Power and Market: Government and the Economy,* Institute for Humane Studies, Menlo Park, California, 1970, pp. 74–5.

proceeds as it does now, there is something sadly inadequate about the idea of saving as postponed consumption.'[4]

This is fully consistent with (b) and (c) above as well as with (a). Simons is right to say that saving may have a value independent of the additional consumption it makes possible. Saving that is never spent is saving in perpetuity.

Saving in perpetuity

The concept of permanent saving has been discussed by the author elsewhere.[5] Saving is permanent if the capital is never spent. Consumption of the capital is not merely deferred but permanently forgone. Forgone permanently, not irrevocably: saving does not acquire its quality of permanence at the outset or irrevocably but becomes permanent merely by virtue of being left undrawn for ever. The original act of saving is thus continually renewed. The saver enjoys not only the reality of receiving the income the saving generates but also the possibility of drawing down the capital as well. But if the saving is permanent, this possibility is never realised.

The concept of permanent saving is perhaps easiest to understand in the aggregate. Even in a stationary economy the use of capital in the production process requires the existence of a permanent pool of savings if the means of production are privately owned. But there are two separate reasons why saving may be permanent individually as well as in the aggregate.

The first is that the saver may indeed intend his saving to be 'a

---

4   *Personal Income Taxation*, op. cit., pp. 95–7.

5   See note 2 on p. 51.

possession for all time'.[6] 'A good man leaveth an inheritance to his children's children,' says Solomon;[7] 'children's children' does not mean grandchildren but remote posterity.[8] Try telling Solomon that 'no one wants capital goods for their own sake ... they are simply the road to future consumption', and so forth.

The second reason is that saving creates wealth by double counting. The same money works twice, once for the borrower and once for the lender. Borrower and lender may be the same person, as in the owner occupation of unmortgaged property; but the argument is the same whether they are or not.

The saver enjoys the wealth as well as the income it produces so long as he is free to spend the principal; spending power is preferred to spending itself. But if access to the principal is restricted, the restrictions themselves reduce its value, even where there is no desire to spend. There is an analogy with fractional banking. As long as all customers are free to draw their money out of the bank, only a small proportion of the maximum is drawn and the remainder is preferred to cash – a situation that can be stable indefinitely.[9] But if the bank's creditworthiness comes under suspicion, the customers' fear that they no longer

---

6   'A possession for all time and not merely the exploit of a passing hour' is the expression applied by Thucydides to his own *History* (I.22).

7   Proverbs xiii, 22.

8   'Visiting the iniquity of the fathers upon the children, and upon the children's children, unto the third and to the fourth generation' (Exodus xxxiv, 7); 'But the mercy of the Lord is from everlasting to everlasting upon them that fear him, and his righteousness unto children's children' (Psalm ciii, 17).

9   This argument is not invalidated by the criticism in some quarters that fractional banking causes inflation. It is sufficient for the analogy that wealth is destroyed by a threat to the power to encash, even though this power is little exercised unless it is threatened.

have the power to encash on demand makes them prefer cash to credit. The run on the bank is caused by their fear of no longer being able to do something they do not wish to do if they are confident that they can.

CHAPTER 5, ANNEX A

TWO FORMS OF PROSPERITY

In Diagram 2 the vertical axis measures wealth and the horizontal axis measures spending.

Economy A, or its average inhabitant, has wealth of 100 and spending of 2. Economy B, or its average inhabitant, has wealth of 50 and spending of 4. It may be assumed for the sake of simplicity that all income is spent and new saving is zero.

The slopes of AC and BD are the reciprocals of the respective yields. AE and BF are indifference curves. The diagram is drawn symmetrically, so that X, where AC cuts BD, and Y, where AE cuts BF, are both on the 45° line.[1] The slope of the straight line AB (not drawn) is the average of the slopes of AC and BD.

At point Y, A and B have the same wealth and the same spending. Above and to the left of Y, wealth increases and spending falls. A is willing to accept a larger reduction in spending than B in return for the same increase in wealth. Below and to the right of Y, wealth decreases and spending rises. B is willing to accept a larger reduction in wealth than A in return for the same increase in spending.

The prosperity of A is measured by a series of lines parallel to AC from the origin outwards. The prosperity of B is measured

---

1   If XY is steeper than the 45° line, the combined income elasticities of demand for wealth exceed the combined income elasticities of demand for spending, and contrariwise if XY is less steep than the 45° line.

Diagram 2   **Two forms of prosperity**

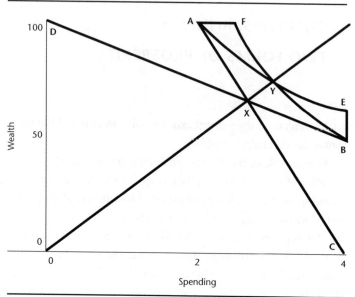

similarly by a series of lines parallel to BD. At point A, the wealth/spending ratio is tangential to the indifference curve AE: wealth of 100 and spending of 2 are the least-cost combination of attaining the indifference curve AE. Similarly, wealth of 50 and spending of 4 are for B the least-cost combination of attaining the indifference curve BF.

It is not possible to say that either A or B is more prosperous than the other. Each has the best position consistent with the respective yield (or ratio of spending to wealth). The yield is lower in A than in B and so the opportunity cost of wealth in terms of spending is lower; it is therefore logical to have a larger ratio of wealth to spending.

AF measures the gain of A relatively to B (or the loss of B relatively to A) as wealth increases from Y to AF. BE measures the gain of B relatively to A (or the loss of A relatively to B) as spending increases from Y to BE.

The best position is for A to be at A and B to be at B. If policy seeks to maximise spending and ignores or underemphasises wealth, it will seek to push A towards B and count such a move a success instead of the failure it really is. The loss inflicted on A by a move to B is measured by BE.

CHAPTER 5, ANNEX B

TAXPAYER RESPONSE TO TAXATION

This annex discusses the variety and extent of rational tax-payer response as a rate of tax rises from zero to a prohibitive level (at which the consumption of the good or service falls to a negligible level or to nothing). The same analysis is used for taxes on goods and services, labour earnings, new saving, ownership for use, ownership in perpetuity, giving for use, giving in perpetuity.[1]

Consider first the simplest example, an *excise duty on spending*.[2] If the excise duty is levied on whisky, the volume purchased is the number of bottles of a given size and specification and the turnover is the amount spent to buy these bottles. At point A in diagram 3, tax is zero. During Stage 1, as the rate of tax rises from A to B, the taxpayer increases not only his turnover but the volume purchased; at B, volume purchased is maximised and this apparently perverse result is discussed in the next paragraph. At point B, the curves of turnover and tax revenue have the same slope. During Stage 2, as the rate of tax rises from B to C, turnover rises but volume purchased falls. C is the point of unitary price elasticity, or maximum turnover, where turnover neither rises nor falls in re-

---

1 Parts of the argument are explained in more detail in *The Taxation of Industry*, op. cit., Appendix v.

2 Excise duties vary from one commodity to another. The argument is the same if value-added tax is added to excise duty: what counts is the total tax on the commodity concerned.

Diagram 3 **Taxpayer response to taxation**

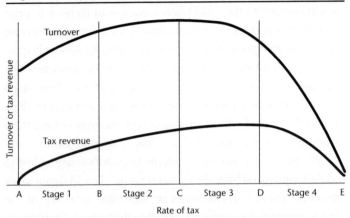

sponse to a rise in the rate of tax. During Stage 3, as the rate of tax rises from C to D, turnover falls but tax revenue continues to rise; D is the point of maximum tax yield. During Stage 4, as the rate of tax rises from D to E, turnover and tax revenue both fall; at E, the point of tax prohibition, turnover and tax revenue have fallen to nothing. B is the point of maximum volume, C is the point of maximum turnover and D is the point of maximum revenue yield.

Points A and B may coincide and generally do so. If B exceeds A, the commodity concerned is a Giffen good, named after the nineteenth-century economist Robert Giffen, who first identified the phenomenon and illustrated it with the example of bread in England. At that time, bread was such an important part of English workers' expenditure that the income effect of a rise in price outweighed the price effect: they had to economise on more expensive foods and increase their consumption of bread. In the twentieth century, Duesenberry, Veblen and others noticed that the very different category of fashion goods is for very different reasons subject to the same phenomenon – an increase in price may effect an increase in quantity purchased (because an increase in price is wrongly regarded as indicating an improvement in quality). There may be other examples. But labour earnings, new saving, ownership and giving are not among them. There is no rational argument for responding to an increase in the tax on these financial magnitudes by increasing the volume acquired. For these magnitudes A coincides with B, and Stage 1 does not exist.

We assume for simplicity that the taxpayer's financial loss in tax paid equals and balances the tax revenue's financial gain in tax received.[3] Taxation also imposes an additional social loss on the private sector of the economy by altering the pattern of activity. At Point C, the point of constant turnover,[4] the purchasing taxpayer's loss in moving from a more favoured to a less favoured position exactly equals the financial loss he incurs through the rise in the rate of tax; his supplier's social loss is additional. During Stage 3, the purchaser's social loss exceeds his financial loss (the distortionary loss exceeds the loss from the rise in the yield of tax) and, during Stage 4, his financial loss is diminishing.

When we apply the analysis to a rise in the *rate of tax on earnings*, the worker is more usually regarded as a supplier rather than a purchaser, a seller rather than a buyer. However, he and his employer are engaged in an act of trade in which each exchanges one thing for another. In this light, the worker may be regarded as purchasing an income with his labour. His turnover is earnings gross of income tax; his earnings net of income tax are the volume of in-

---

3   In reality the taxpayer's loss exceeds the tax revenue's gain by the sum of the taxpayer's compliance costs and the tax revenue's collection costs.

4   Or unitary price elasticity of demand.

come purchased. Income purchased is neither bread in England nor a fashion good: Points A and B coincide and Stage 1 does not exist. In Stage 2, from B to C, he increases his turnover in order to offset part of the reduction in his standard of living: he works harder, but there is still a fall in his standard of living (the volume of income purchased). During Stage 3, he works less hard and, during Stage 4, he works so much less hard that tax revenue falls as the rate of tax rises. Stage 4 is exemplified in reverse by the rise in tax revenue as very high postwar rates of tax on earned income were reduced in the United Kingdom and the United States.

The argument is similar for *new saving for use*, such as saving for a pension. Turnover is the amount saved and volume is the amount of pension purchased. Stage 1 does not exist; as for earnings, volume always falls. Turnover rises in Stage 2 and falls in Stage 3. Volume, turnover and tax revenue fall in Stage 4.[5]

The argument is different for *new saving in perpetuity*. If the saver is not saving for a particular purpose there is no incentive to save resulting from the imposition of a tax on new saving, whether in the form of a tax on the investment income generated by the new saving or in the form of a tax on its parent capital. There is only a price effect: saving has become more expensive relatively to spending. Since the saver is not seeking to attain a particular standard of

5   The amount of new saving, which in this analysis is turnover, is conventionally (and in this perspective wrongly) treated as the volume of saving. However, the logic of the argument is unaffected. Stage 1 does not exist. During Stage 2, volume, in the sense of the amount saved, rises and tax revenue rises. During Stage 3, the amount saved falls and tax revenue rises. During Stage 4, the amount saved falls and tax revenue falls. The nineteenth-century economist W. L. Sargant is credited with being the first to notice that the turnover of new saving (or volume in the sense of the amount saved) may rise in response to a fall in the yield, whether caused by a rise in the rate of tax or otherwise; this phenomenon is sometimes called the Sargant effect.

living or any other aim as a consumer, it is not rational to respond to this relative price change by disbursing more on saving and thus less on spending. Neither Stage 1 nor Stage 2 exists. Turnover on saving falls and on spending rises. In Stage 3, tax revenue rises but turnover including tax revenue falls. Turnover excluding tax revenue falls faster than tax revenue rises. The distortionary loss exceeds the rise in tax revenue. In Stage 4, both turnover and tax revenue fall.[6]

Thus Stage 2 (rising turnover) exists for new saving for use but not for new saving in perpetuity. The distinction is clear in principle, although it is less precise in practice (since the saver may change his mind at any time).

New saving once made becomes *old saving* or *wealth*. Again, we distinguish between old saving for use and old saving in perpetuity. The concept of old saving for use implies an excess of consumption over income; in other words, a drawing down of capital. The concept of old saving in perpetuity implies that income is not less than consumption. If income exceeds consumption, the excess represents new acts of new saving.

Once savings have been made, they are vulnerable to increases in taxation, which are in the circumstances retrospective. In a *going system*, however, there are no changes in the rules, which are known in advance before the new saving is made. In a going system, there is a distinction between ownership for use and owner-

---

6 By contrast with new saving in perpetuity, a bequest to a particular individual or charity may seek to place a certain net-of-tax sum in the hand of the recipient. The price elasticity of demand for bequeathing may then be less than unitary and the gross-of-tax bequest may rise in response to the tax. (*The Wealth of Giving*, op. cit., pp. 79–84). Although this effect is possible for small legacies constituting the lesser part of an estate, it is hardly conceivable for the remainder-man or the estate in general.

ship in perpetuity corresponding to the similar distinction for new saving. Ownership for use goes through Stage 2, in which turnover rises in response to a tax increase; ownership in perpetuity does not and starts with Stage 3. A tax on ownership in perpetuity, like a tax on new saving in perpetuity, causes a distortionary loss in excess of the tax revenue.

A similar distinction holds good between giving for use and giving in perpetuity. A charitable donor may wish to endow a library; a father may wish to pay for the education of his child. These are examples of giving for use. If the cost of the library or the education increases, whether for tax reasons or otherwise, one of the range of rational responses is for the donor to increase his disbursements. If, by contrast, the gift is untargeted and in perpetuity and a tax is imposed, giving has become more expensive relatively to other uses of money, and it is not rational to increase disbursements for giving. A tax on giving always causes a social loss; and giving has no economic taxable capacity, in the sense that the social loss from a tax on giving always at least equals the revenue yield.[7]

Short of the logical extreme at which the price elasticity of demand is zero and demand is entirely unresponsive to increases in price, all taxes inflict losses through their distortionary effects on the pre-tax pattern of behaviour. The larger the price elasticity of demand, the larger the distortionary loss. This annex has argued that perpetual saving, owning and giving are a destructive basis for taxation since (by contrast with most other taxes) the distortionary effect of even a low rate of tax exceeds the revenue yield. The distortionary effect measures the loss caused by a tax-induced

---

7   See p. 47 above.

move from a preferred to a less-favoured pattern of activity. But the damage goes farther. For giving, in perpetuity or otherwise, the social loss caused by the destruction of donor's countervalue and surplus always at least equals the revenue yield. For saving and ownership in perpetuity, the loss to the saver or owner caused by a tax-induced move from a preferred to a less-favoured pattern is matched by a loss to the rest of society, which under perpetual saving enjoys the use of the perpetual saver's funds without any effective obligation to repay.

CHAPTER 7, ANNEX A

THE MEANINGS OF EQUALITY

What I have called *totalitarian equality* is a comparatively recent statistical concept. It is the opposite of *inequality*, for which a variety of measures (generally with a minimum of zero and a maximum of unity) were devised at about the time of World War I.[1] These measures purport to compute the variations in a particular characteristic over the whole of a population, in the common or statistical sense of that term.

Equality in this totalitarian sense means strictly *perfect equality* or *total equality*, of which history provides few, if any, examples in human society. In practice, totalitarian equality means something like *acceptable* or *lower* or *declining* inequality.

Economic equality is further classified into equality of *opportunity* and equality of *outcome*. We are not here concerned with equality of opportunity. Strictly interpreted, this would require a very oppressive control of people's lives. When qualified and modified, equality of opportunity comes to no more than the widely acceptable idea that everyone should have a *good, satisfactory or adequate* start in life or an opportunity to *exploit his talents*.

The social ideal of equality of outcomes bristles with difficulties. A number of the principal ambiguities and contradictions are discussed in Annex B. But overarching all these particular difficulties is a more general problem. Totalitarian equality is an inescapably statistical concept. All other notions of right and wrong, obligation and proscription, are intelligible to the innumerate. All other notions concern, or can be broken down into, dealings with individuals. Only equality concerns the simultaneous interrelationships of everyone with everyone else. Similarly, other concepts of obligation specify that this is right, that is wrong, this is better, that is worse. Only equality posits the best in terms of an indefinable compromise between two unacceptables, maximum and minimum inequality. There is no way of identifying the most acceptable or least unacceptable degree of inequality that is not wholly arbitrary and subjective.

We now turn to the non-totalitarian or human-scale ideas of equality, starting with the Greek word for equality, *isotes*.

Isotes

When Jocasta says

> Better, my son, to honour Equality,
> Which binds friends for ever to friends,
> Cities to cities and allies to allies[2]

she is using the term in the sense of fair and honest dealings between neighbours. Plato says that 'the truest and best equality is no longer easy for everyone to identify. For it is the judgment of Zeus ... for it grants more to the greater and less to the smaller,

---

1   Costantino Bresciani-Turroni (1909, 1916); Hugh Dalton (1920); Otto Dunkel (1909); Corrado Gini (1912, 1914, 1930); M. O. Lorenz (1905); Giorgio Mortara (1910); Warren Persons (1909); Gaetano Pietra (1914); Umberto Ricci (1915, 1916); G. P. Watkins (1909); Dwight B. Yntema (1933); Allyn A. Young (1917). See References.

2   Euripides, *The Phoenician Women*, 535.

giving each man what is due to him by nature';[3] this concept of distributive justice is the opposite of totalitarian equality. Similarly, Aristotle says that 'equality has a dual nature, one numerical, the other according to worth'.[4] Menander has *isotes* in the sense of fair dealing or impartiality.[5] Polybius speaks of equality between members of the Achaean League, in the sense that there were no privileges for the original members over those joining later.[6]

Inequality is not a biblical word; nor are *share* or *sharing*. St Paul speaks of *equality* on two occasions. II Corinthians viii, 14 reads: 'But by an equality, that now at this time your abundance may be a supply for their want, that their abundance also may be a supply for your want: that there may be equality', which is a concept of reciprocal self-help or mutuality. Colossians iv, 1 reads: 'Masters, give unto your servants that which is just and equal', where the concept is one of justice or fair dealing and economic equality is precluded by the context.

Equality

Equality is used little, if at all, in the totalitarian statistical sense before the twentieth century. Adam Smith, in *The Wealth of Nations*,[7] uses the term in the sense of *proportionality* or what would now be called *horizontal equity* (the like treatment of taxpayers in similar situations). Similarly McCulloch, in the Introduction to *Taxation*

---

3   *Laws* vi, 757 B-C.

4   *Politics*, 1302a, 7. Aristotle's term for *equality* here is *ison*, not *isotes*.

5   *Single verses*, 259. Hugh Dalton's citation of Menander in *Some aspects of the inequality of incomes in modern communities* (George Routledge and Sons, London, 1925) in the totalitarian sense of an equal income distribution is anachronistic.

6   *Histories*, ii, 38, 8.

7   v, ii, ii.

(1852), says that 'Equality is of the essence of such taxes', by which he means proportionality.

Pre-statistical senses of *equality* cited by the Oxford English Dictionary include: the condition of having equal dignity, rank or privileges with others; the condition of being equal in power, ability, achievement or excellence; fairness, impartiality, equity; equability.

CHAPTER 7, ANNEX B

THE AMBIGUITIES OF EQUALITY

Equality not only has different meanings or senses; the different meanings have varying interpretations. These ambiguities of equality are the subject of the present annex.

Whether two or more persons are equal or not may be judged by different and conflicting criteria. The Christian doctrine of the Trinity provides a notable example. Arianism was and is the most subversive of the major heresies: if Christ is not fully God, he is soon little more than an exceptional man, which is what many non-Christians believe him to be. Hence the insistence of St Athanasius that 'in this Trinity none is afore, or after other: none is greater, or less than another' (Athanasian Creed). The Proper Preface for Trinity Sunday says: 'For that which we believe of the glory of the Father, the same we believe of the Son, and of the Holy Ghost, without any difference or inequality.' Yet there are texts apparently at variance with these robust assertions. Christ says: 'my Father is greater than I' (John xiv, 28).[1] Christ also speaks of 'the Comforter, whom I will send unto you from the Father' (John xv, 26); and he who sends is normally greater and he who is sent, lesser. Thus the Christian doctrine of equality between the Persons of the Trinity has to accommodate these appearances to the contrary.

---

1   This was a sore point with St Basil, who describes those who use this expression as 'graceless creatures, offspring of the Evil One' (Letter viii).

The three Persons of the Trinity are portrayed in the Bible as having different roles or activities; and the difficulties inherent in the concept of equality between them are a pattern for the ambiguities involved in assessing the existence or even desirability of equality between two or more human agents (or the means by which this equality may or may not be achievable). A number of the more important ambiguities are discussed briefly in the section on dimensions below.

The dimensions of equality

1 *Equality of opportunity or outcome?* Equality of opportunity, itself a totalitarian and oppressive concept, is compatible with substantial inequality of outcome.

2 *Snapshot or lifetime inequality?* An economy in which individuals were completely equal over their lifetimes might nevertheless have substantial inequality at any one moment.

3 *Changing places.* If A is much more prosperous than B in period 1 and B is equivalently more prosperous than A in period 2, is the inequality between them zero or substantially positive? This is not the same as the distinction between snapshot and lifetime inequality, since snapshot inequality may be due to variations within a lifetime cycle that is common to all.

4 *Equality between whom?* Since substantial inequality within families is normal, inequality between families is less than inequality between individuals.

5 *Ideals and derogations.* Complete equality is sometimes presented as an ideal, from which derogations are unfortunately required for practical reasons. The best policy is thus a compromise (seldom or never identified statistically) between complete equality and the

distribution determined by freely chosen exchanges between buyers and sellers. The opposite ideal is not complete inequality (winner takes all) but the distribution of the market, derogations from which take the form of taxation and other types of government interference.

6 *Inequality of wealth or income or consumption?* These different concepts of inequality lead in different (and inconsistent) policy directions. These inconsistencies are discussed on p. 79 above, under the heading 'The over-determination of policy'. Lifestyles of rich and poor are much more similar in Britain at the beginning of the 21st century than they were a hundred or two hundred years earlier; and this would be reflected in a decline of inequality if it were measured in terms of spending. In practice, the measure is usually based on income or wealth, which much exaggerates the inequality of lifestyles.

7 *Inequality gross or net of tax?* Since richer people are generally taxed more heavily than poorer people, the degree of inequality is also exaggerated if the statistical computation is based on gross-of-tax income or wealth instead of net. The inequality of wealth is always based on gross-of-tax figures, since the tax liabilities, although substantial, are difficult to compute or can be computed in different ways. The inequality of income is computed both gross of tax and net; but gross measures predominate.

8 *Welfare services.* Tawney[2] and others have recommended the provision of welfare services by the government free at the point of

---

2   In *Equality*, George Allen and Unwin, London, 1951 ed., Epilogue (ii). This was also a theme of Simons more than ten years earlier: 'Opportunities for extending the scope of socialized consumption are clearly numerous ... governmental bodies might, on a moderate scale, function quite as well as the investment departments of the better banks and insurance companies' (*Personal Income Taxation*, op. cit., p. 27).

consumption as a means of reducing inequality. This is open to certain objections: first, that it is inefficient, as trucking[3] is inefficient, because it replaces money with services provided in kind without freedom of exit; and second, that inequality may be increased rather than reduced by the phenomenon of middle-class capture: better-educated and more articulate citizens can turn the system to their advantage and, in particular, free or subsidised university education means a substantial transfer to the middle class from poorer fellow-citizens.

9 *Inequality and poverty.* Some look at inequality from the perspective of reducing absolute poverty. In this perspective, what is important is the relation of the lowest tenth or quarter (decile or quartile) of the population to the rest; the distribution within the upper nine-tenths or three-quarters is less important or unimportant. This idea has respectable antecedents and credentials (although there is always a potential threat from moral hazard, the corruption of the recipient of state largesse through the erosion of his incentives to work and save). It is really about the relief of poverty. It has not much to do with inequality, although it can be clad in egalitarian garb through the use of sufficiently way-out measures of inequality, as we note in the section on 'The measures of inequality' below.

10 *Inequality and riches.* Some take the opposite line and look at inequality from the perspective of reducing riches. This is the perspective that effectively governs tax policy at present. The poor must take their chance, and what happens to the majority of the population is their concern. The problem is inordinate riches.

---

3   Trucking was the payment of employees otherwise than in money and often in vouchers exchangeable at the employer's shops. It was forbidden by the Truck Acts of 1831 and 1870.

Now, in any large statistical population there are bound to be outliers. Since zero is the minimum (except for the self-employed, who may make losses), outliers in an income distribution are bound to lie upwards. In this egalitarian perspective, upward outliers are acceptable provided that no element of personal merit is involved: wins from lotteries and football pools are untaxed in the hands of the winners, but income or gains from earning, saving or enterprise are taxed heavily. Inheritance tax and capital gains tax on individuals bring in derisory sums to the Revenue; but they inflict huge damage on the tiny proportion of taxpayers that is subject to their charge. They inflict further damage on the economy and the tax revenue itself, when account is taken of the activities that move away in search of a less oppressive tax regime.

Like sympathy for poverty, the animus against riches may be dressed in statistical garb as a seeking for equality. Measures of inequality exist which flatter this proclivity. Measures of inequality are the subject of the next section.

The measures of inequality

The various measures of inequality are compared and contrasted in detail in Appendix I of my book *The Measurement of Fiscal Policy*[4] (hereafter MFP Appendix I).

MFP Appendix I shows that there is an infinite variety of measures of inequality – in other words, there is no limit to the number of different ways in which inequality can be measured. Dimensions of this variation include the following: (a) inequality can be measured ordinally (by means of percentiles) or cardinally

---

4   Op. cit.

(by means of the absolute values of each member of the distribution); (b) cardinal measures may or may not have lower and upper limits such as zero and unity; (c) cardinal measures may compare members of the distribution with each other or with a measure of location such as the arithmetic mean or average; (d) the differences or deviations from which the measure of inequality is computed may be simple numbers or powers of those numbers such as squares or cubes, the corresponding root of the sum being taken: the use of powers overemphasises extreme values and underemphasises central values.

A distribution that is more unequal than another by one measure of inequality may be less unequal by another measure. There is no unequivocal statistical measure of inequality. The *reversal ratio* between any two statistical measures of inequality gives the maximum ratio of the inequality of two distributions under one measure that is compatible with their reversal under the other measure. Thus a distribution may be twice as unequal as another under one measure and yet less unequal under the other. Reversal ratios are computed for a number of different pairs of measures in MFP Appendix I, Tables 23, 25, pp. 111–13.

There is no upper limit to reversal ratios. In other words, however large the initial difference between distributions, another statistical measure of inequality can always be found to reverse the order, so that one distribution is more unequal than the other by one measure and less unequal by the other.

Many people accept some forms of inequality but reject others: they accept the pomp of rulers, for example, but reject the wealth of rich merchants. Other people may reject extremes of wealth or poverty while remaining indifferent to distribution or redistribution within a middle class comprising the greater part of the population. A statistical measure of inequality can generally or always be found which reflects such preferences or prejudices within its basis of computation. Thus Allyn Young, in using the term *concentration* to mean 'undue or excessive' inequality, is implicitly recommending the use of higher-power coefficients and thus counting a given amount of inequality twice or three times or more.[5]

MFP Appendix I argues against the higher-power coefficients on the ground that they confuse inequality with secondary characteristics of a distribution such as skewness. The preferred measures in MFP are the Gini coefficient (corresponding to the Lorenz curve), which compares each member of a distribution with all other members, and the simple unit mean deviation coefficient (simple in the sense of being computed from ordinary numbers and not from higher powers of these numbers). In the perspective of the present monograph, the Gini coefficient is the statistical handmaid of totalitarian envy, which invites every member of the population to envy all other members. It has the additional disadvantage that its method of computation is too complex to be intelligible to most ordinary people. Despite its advantages for purely statistical purposes, its use in political contexts imposes a heavy cost.

The simple unit mean deviation coefficient (SUMDC) is the easiest measure to understand and compute. It is the sum of deviations from the arithmetic mean (regardless of sign), divided by the product of the mean (M) and the number in the population (N). The formula is

---

5   *Do the Statistics of the Concentration of Wealth in the United States Mean What They Are Commonly Assumed to Mean?*, Publications of the American Statistical Association, 1917.

$$\frac{\Sigma|M-X|}{NM}$$

It follows that redistributions within the sections of the population above or below the arithmetic mean leave this coefficient of inequality unchanged. This is shown in Table 1, where a total of 30 is divided between three people (I, II and III) and the arithmetic mean is therefore 10.

In situations A–C of Table 1, redistributions below the arithmetic mean and in D and E redistributions above the arithmetic mean leave the coefficient unchanged. In the move from A to F, the redistribution from II to III crosses the arithmetic mean, and so the coefficient rises to .40. In G and H, there is a redistribution between (I) and (II) which leaves the coefficient unchanged at .40. In I and J, the coefficient is also unchanged after a redistribution between (II) and (III).

The same point is put differently by Blum and Kalven. 'As long as there are at least three income classes', they say,[6] 'the fundamental ambiguity remains, and it is still necessary to decide whether, in stopping short of absolute equality, the objective is to bring the bottom and top closer together' (situation F to C in Table 1) 'or bring more persons closer to the top' (situation F to A) 'or more persons closer to the bottom' (situation I to D). The fall in the coefficient of inequality (the SUMDC) is the same for all these three changes.

Thus the ambiguities of the concept of equality or inequality extend from the field of its operation to the method of its mea-

---

6   *The Uneasy Case for Progressive Taxation*, op. cit., p. 98.

Table 1 **The unit mean deviation coefficient (UMDC)**

Situation	I	II	III	$\Sigma|M-X|$	UMDC
A	5	10	15	10	.33
B	5.5	9.5	15	10	.33
C	6	9	15	10	.33
D	5	11	14	10	.33
E	5	12	13	10	.33
F	5	9	16	12	.40
G	6	8	16	12	.40
H	7	7	16	12	.40
I	4	12	14	12	.40
J	4	13	13	12	.40

surement. No one coefficient can be expected to reveal the whole truth about the dispersion of a distribution of many members or even as few as three members, each of which may vary independently of all the others. It is an advantage, not a disadvantage, of the SUMDC that it does not pass the transfer test (in other words, it may be unaffected by transfers from one member of the population to another). It emphasises the amount of deviation from the average, both above and below, and ignores transfers within the richer and poorer groups which leave the amount of deviation unaffected. But although the UMDC may be the best or least bad measure of inequality, the concept of inequality itself has serious deficiencies as a political ideal, because in many of its senses it has no close connection with serious policy aims like the reduction of poverty, and it may even operate in the opposite direction.

CHAPTER 7, ANNEX C

INEQUALITIES OF WEALTH AND SPENDING

We saw in Chapter 5 how inheritance tax cheapens the rich man's spending: in a consistent or *going* tax system (one without changes or uncompleted effects of earlier changes), the effect of inheritance tax, certain in theory and likely in practice, is to increase the inequality of spending by increasing the spending of the rich relatively to that of the poor. This perverse distributive consequence is illustrated in Table 2, where the income elasticity of demand for saving in perpetuity is assumed to be greater than unity. The inequality of spending rises because there is a proportionately larger increase in the spending of the wealthier taxpayers.

Since lifetime giving is normally from richer to poorer, the frustration of this giving through taxation may also cause a rise in the inequality of wealth.

Even if the inequality of spending is reduced initially by a new tax on saving, it is increased eventually. The inequality of spending falls initially as the tax on saving (for example, death duties) reduces the stock of wealth existing at the time of its introduction and the income generated by this stock. As time goes by, new saving becomes more and more important relatively to the pre-tax stock of saving: there is an asymptotic approach of total new savings to total savings, including the remnants of the stock of pre-tax savings. At this point the inequality of spending rises. This is illustrated in Table 3, which compares the pre-tax Situation 1 with the

Table 2 **Anti-sumptuary taxation**[1]

		A	B	C
No tax on saving				
i	Income	100	200	300
ii	Saving in perpetuity	10	30	60
iii	Spending	90	170	240
Prohibitive tax on saving				
iv	Saving in perpetuity	–	–	–
v	Income/spending	100	200	300
vi	Increase in spending	10	30	60
vii	Original spending	90	170	240

Table 3 **The effect on inequality of a tax on saving**[2]

	Situation 1		Situation 2	
	A	B	A	B
Capital	1,000	100	800	100
Income	50	5	40	5
Spending	30	5	40	5

eventual post-tax Situation 2. The inequality of wealth falls, the richer taxpayer stops saving and the inequality of spending rises.

I have shown elsewhere that in the absence of the Sargant effect (an increase in saving to offset an increase in taxes on saving) all taxes on saving increase the inequality of spending.[3]

---

1   Table 2 appeared in *Is Inheritance Legitimate?*, op. cit., p. 195.

2   Table 3 appeared in *Is Inheritance Legitimate?*, op. cit., p. 196.

3   *The Taxation of Industry*, op. cit., Appendix III.

CHAPTER 7, ANNEX D
OF CAKES AND SLICES

Diagram 4 shows the division of output between two individuals, X and Y. Y has more wealth, income and expenditure than X. The two circles represent outputs of different sizes. By definition, outputs sum to the same total as inputs and income is the sum of expenditure and new saving. Output is reduced by tax increases and increased by tax reductions. Taxes rise and fall proportionately more for Y than for X. Taxes may be levied on income (from earnings and investments) or on outgo (expenditure plus new saving).

In Situations (1) and (2), outgo is the sum of expenditure and (new) temporary saving (like saving for a holiday or a pension). In Situation (1), X has (I + II) and Y has III. Taxes are reduced and output increases. In Situation (2), X has (I + IV) and Y has (II + III + V + VI). Y has a larger slice of a larger cake. X loses proportionately; he loses absolutely if II > IV and gains absolutely if IV > II. The argument is the same in reverse for tax increases.

In Situations (3) and (4), outgo is the sum of expenditure (including the present value of eventual expenditure out of temporary saving) and saving in perpetuity. In Situation (3), X has I and Y has (II + III). In Situation (4), Y transfers a slice of his outgo from expenditure to saving in perpetuity, which is now taxed less heavily. His consumption is (III + VI); his saving in perpetuity is (II + V), a total increase of (V + VI). If II > VI, his expenditure

Diagram 4   **The cake and the slice**

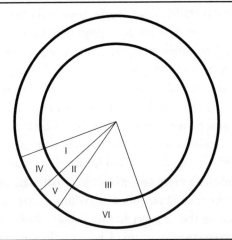

falls; if VI > II, his expenditure rises. (II + V), Y's saving in perpetuity, works twice. It works once for Y as owner and a second time for X as user. Y has the ownership of these resources, X enjoys their use. X's outgo is (I + II + IV + V), an increase of IV (increased expenditure) plus (II + V), which is the use of Y's saving in perpetuity.

If the incentive effects of tax reduction are ignored or assumed to be zero, there are not two circles but only one. Total output is unaffected by tax changes; IV, V and VI fall away. As taxes rise, II is transferred from Y to X; as taxes fall, II is transferred from X to Y. This must result if output is unchanged and a redistributive tax on Y is increased or reduced. This is possible if II is a mixture of expenditure and temporary saving; but it is implausible or impossible if II is saving in perpetuity, owned by Y and used by X, and subject to a higher redistributive tax. If output is unchanged, (I +

II + III) is unchanged. Y's income falls, so (II + III) falls. The fall in Y's income is entirely due to the increase in the tax on saving in perpetuity. Saving in perpetuity is dearer, the price of spending is unchanged. The rational response is to compensate for the increase in the price of saving in perpetuity by shifting to consumption. III increases; so II falls more than (II + III). I increases by the fall in (II + III). (I + II) falls by the increase in III. At the logical extreme, III is unchanged and I increases by the fall in II; otherwise (I + II) falls. This is the logical extreme because saving in perpetuity is not a Giffen good, the demand for which rises as its price increases. Only temporary saving is subject to the Sargant effect (an increase in the amount expended on saving in response to a tax increase, because the taxpayer has to disburse more resources to achieve a given target standard of living); if the saving is in perpetuity, there is no future standard of living in question, and the Sargant effect cannot operate.

The argument of this annex is thus consistent with the argument of *The Taxation of Industry*, Appendix III that in the absence of the Sargant effect any tax on saving increases the inequality of spending.

This annex has shown that, in so far as taxes bear on saving in perpetuity, there is no trade-off between equity and output. The reduction of these taxes reduces the inequality of expenditure and may reduce inequality overall; in Diagram 4, it will reduce inequality overall if $(IV + II + V) / I > (V + VI) / (II + III)$.[1]

---

1   In this sense, overall inequality is based on the sum of spending and the use or ownership of saving in perpetuity. Other senses of overall inequality discussed in *The Taxation of Industry*, Appendix III (pp. 134–6), are the inequality of (a) income net of income tax, (b) income gross of income tax, (c) outgo net of taxes on saving and spending, (d) spending and wealth combined.

CHAPTER 8, ANNEX A

SAME-SEX UNIONS: THE LAW AROUND THE WORLD

Belgium

A law passed in March gives gay couples inheritance rights and allows them to open joint bank accounts.

Canada

1998 court rulings insist that gay couples be given the same pension rights as straight couples. The provinces affected are not appealing the ruling. See the Federation for Equal Families website for more information. Gay groups have launched a lawsuit demanding an overhaul of 58 laws to bring the law into line with the charter of freedoms. Ottawa has decided to proceed with amendments that will treat homosexual couples the same as heterosexuals in everything from pensions to bankruptcy laws, government sources told the *Globe and Mail*. Unfortunately, Prime Minister Chrétien has denied it.

Denmark

In 1989 Denmark became the first country in the world to allow same-sex marriages. In 2000, Denmark passed a law that gives homosexual couples the right to obtain custody of children by a previous heterosexual marriage; however, gay couples still cannot adopt children.

Germany

The new centre-left government intends to grant some legal status to same-sex couples, but not the right to adopt children.

Hungary

Hungary passed a law in 1996 granting gay couples inheritance rights; but the law doesn't allow adoptions. Hungary's situation results from a legal case that applied the European Charter (more for political reasons [fear of not being accepted into the EU] than anything else) and ruled in favour of same-sex relationships. The status of gays is probably broader than just pension rights.

Iceland

Iceland approved *registered cohabitation* in 1996, giving gay couples many of the legal rights enjoyed by heterosexual married couples, with the exception of adoption.

Netherlands

A new law took effect in 1999 permitting gay and lesbian couples to marry, giving them the same pension, social security and inheritance rights as other married couples. The Dutch Cabinet approved a plan in November 1999 to let homosexuals adopt children. The adoption bill places some restrictions on foreign adoptions. Gay couples of either sex will have the option of being married or being domestic partners. The proposal became law in September 2000. Gays gained access to full marriage in January 2001 under the same laws as apply to opposite-sex couples. Couples who previously registered under the partnership law are allowed to convert their unions to ordinary marriage.

Norway

Same-sex marriage is legal and has been called Registered Domestic Partnership since 1 August 1993. The regime is virtually the same in Sweden and Denmark. It can be used for mental patient commitment. The Norwegian Church does not allow church marriages, but it is very influential as it is a state Church, and it supported the passage, though there is a rural backlash which has caused a Church schism. Apparently, as of 1997, there were 700 registered partnerships in a country of 4.3 million with 850,000 married. Registrations run at about 100 per year. The legislation passed by only one vote, and a Norwegian representative named Anders Gasland came out just before the vote and his argument about not being able to love was a help in the passage and a courageous thing for him to do. Adoption is still not available as is also the case with in vitro fertilisation. The primary reason adoption is an issue in Europe seems to be the fear that if gays are allowed to adopt it will cause the cut-off of international adoptions from countries with a different view who are currently relied on for a supply of babies.

Sweden

Sweden has allowed homosexuals to register as partners in a form of civil marriage since 1995. The couples cannot adopt children or have them through artificial means. Church weddings are not permitted.

United Kingdom

In July 2000, about 100 British legislators voiced support for efforts to give homosexuals the right to receive the partner's state pension after death.

The above is based on postings to the queerlaw-can-request@egale.ca listserv by Timothy Ross Wilson, tim@timwilson.com, and George T. H. Fuller, loisf@unixg.ubc.ca, as at December 2000.

GLOSSARY

administrative costs of taxation: the sum of compliance costs and collection costs.

asymptotic: approaching a limit more and more closely without ever reaching it.

break-even rate of discount: the rate of discount (between the saver's subjective rate and zero) below which consumption may be regarded as the purpose of saving and above which it cannot.

business property relief: a relief against inheritance tax. At the present 100 per cent rate of relief, qualifying assets are effectively exempt.

capital dimension of prosperity: the economic value provided by privately owned assets otherwise than through their yield.

capital transfer tax: a form of United Kingdom death duties levied on the testator/donor between 1975 and 1986.

collection costs of taxation: the costs incurred by the government/Treasury/Revenue/tax-gatherers.

compliance costs of taxation: the costs imposed on the taxpayer. See *vexation.*

consistent tax system: see *going tax system.*

consumer's surplus: the excess of the money a consumer would be willing to pay for a good or service, rather than go without the amount bought, over what he pays.

costless wealth creation: the creation of economic value without costly inputs.

death duties: a generic term for such imposts as estate duty, capital transfer tax, inheritance tax, succession duty, legacy duty, whether levied on the testator/donor or on the recipient.

dilution (also dispersal, dissipation): ownership dilution, dispersal or dissipation is the destruction of value (or the prevention of its realisation) through the reduction of ownership *intensity.*

donor's countervalue: the utility of a gift to an effective altruist that exactly matches and compensates for his financial loss. If donor's countervalue falls short of the market value of an asset, the altruism is ineffective and the gift is not made. If the utility of a gift to an effective altruist exceeds the market value of the asset, the excess is *donor's surplus.*

donor's surplus: the excess of the utility of a gift to an effective altruist over the market value of the asset concerned.

economic distortion: see *excess burden.*

economic taxable capacity: the excess of the yield of a tax over the social loss it inflicts (exclusive of the yield). In other words, the excess of the yield over the *excess burden.*

enjoyment: the sum of the capital dimension of prosperity and the yield.

estate duty: a form of United Kingdom death duties levied on the testator/donor between 1894 and 1975.

excess burden: the burden (additional to the yield of tax) of fiscal interference with economic decisions and distortion of efficient choice.

existence value: the value to owner or non-owner created by the knowledge of the existence of something which itself has value.

farmers' paradox: the consequence of capital taxation whereby a rise in the value of an asset which apparently makes a taxpayer richer makes him in reality poorer if its value to him exceeds the new higher price. Relevant assets include farms, firms, stocks and shares. Death duties expose the taxpayer to the double jeopardy (or double lottery) of unexpected death at a time when asset values are high.

fashion goods: luxury goods for which the demand increases rather than falls as a result of an increase in price. See *Giffen goods.*

Giffen goods: necessary goods for which the demand increases rather than falls as a result of an increase in price. See *fashion goods.*

gifts inter vivos: gifts made during the donor's lifetime.

Gini coefficient: simple unit mean difference coefficient of concentration (inequality). The Gini coefficient compares each member of a distribution or population with all other members. See *Lorenz curve, simple unit mean deviation coefficient (SUMDC).*

going tax system: a system in which there are no changes and the effects of past changes have worked through. Also known as a *consistent tax system.*

gross rate of tax: a tax-inclusive rate, levied on a base including the tax. Thus gross-of-tax income 100, tax 20, net-of-tax income 80, gross tax rate 20 per cent.

heriot: a medieval form of death duty consisting of a nominally voluntary donation from a tenant to his feudal lord.

horizontal equity: a principle of fiscal justice that is satisfied when taxpayers in like circumstances are taxed alike.

income effect: the reduction in a taxpayer's net-of-tax income caused by a tax or a tax increase.

inheritance tax: a form of United Kingdom death duties levied on the testator/donor from 1986.

intension: the measure of tax graduation or 'progressiveness' proposed in *The Measurement of Fiscal Policy*.[1]

intensity: the opposite of dilution. Ownership intensity is the creation or preservation of value through an articulated system of property rights enabling assets to be owned by an individual or a small number of individuals (such as a family) or a larger but still limited number of individuals with close ties of interest, affection or belief (such as a religious house or order, regiment or college).

legacy duty: a form of death duties usually charged on the recipient.

lifetime cumulation of transfers: a characteristic of capital transfer tax between 1975 and 1981 whereby the tax base was the total of transfers made by the donor/testator during his lifetime and on his death.

Lorenz curve: diagrammatic representation of the *Gini coefficient*.

net rate of tax: a tax-exclusive rate, a rate levied on a base excluding the tax. Thus net-of-tax expenditure 100, tax 25, cost to consumer 125, net tax rate 25 per cent (= 25/100), corresponding gross tax rate 20 per cent (= 25/125).

price effect: the increase in the price of a good or service to the taxpayer caused by a tax or a tax increase.

'progressive' taxation: 'progressive' or graduated taxation taxes richer taxpayers proportionately more than poorer.

public good: a good or service the use or enjoyment of which by one person does not reduce the amount available for use or

---

1   op. cit.

enjoyment by others. An example is the wealth created by personal giving.[2]

reversal ratio: the maximum ratio of the inequalities of two distributions or populations under one measure of inequality that is compatible with a reversal of the order under another measure (the more unequal becoming the less unequal and vice versa).[3]

Sargant effect: an increase in disbursements on saving in response to a reduction in the yield, whether tax-induced or otherwise, or a reduction in disbursements in response to an increase. The taxpayer is attempting to reach a target level of income from investment.

saving in perpetuity (perpetual saving): saving that is never realised for consumption, whether by accident or design.

secondary gains or losses: the consequences of a tax increase or reduction for the yields of other taxes. Secondary changes are normally opposite in sign from primary changes.

simple unit mean deviation coefficient (SUMDC): the sum of the positive and negative deviations from the arithmetic mean, taken irrespective of sign, divided by the product of the mean and the number of the population.

social loss: a reduction in the money or money's worth available to government or individuals in aggregate resulting from a change in economic activity or policy.

succession duty: a form of death duties, usually charged on the recipient.

sumptuary taxation: a system taxing goods and services typically

---

2   *The Wealth of Giving*, op. cit., p. 61.

3   *The Measurement of Fiscal Policy*, op. cit., Appendix i F.

purchased by the rich proportionately more than those
purchased by the poor.

tax wedge: see *excess burden.*

temporary saving: saving that is eventually realised for
consumption. Examples are saving for Christmas, saving for a
holiday, saving for a pension annuity.

trucking: the payment of employees otherwise than in money, in
particular in vouchers exchangeable at the employer's shops.

unitary price elasticity: relationship between price and demand
yielding constancy of disbursements (turnover) as prices vary.

use: enjoyment of an asset through occupation or handling and
not merely through the pleasure of ownership.

vertical inequity: a form of fiscal injustice whereby the poorer
taxpayer incurs the heavier tax burden. Inheritance tax and
capital gains tax provide the principal examples.

vexation: non-monetary compliance costs, including the frequent
visits and the odious examinations of the tax-gatherers.

vicesima hereditatium: Roman death duties at 5 per cent (gross).

REFERENCES

Works cited in this monograph

Bentham, Jeremy (1795), *Supply without Burthen, or Escheat vice Taxation*, J. Debrett.

Blum, Walter J., and Harry Kalven, Jr (1953), *The Uneasy Case for Progressive Taxation*, University of Chicago Press, Chicago.

Boswell, James, *Life of Johnson*.

Bracewell-Milnes, Barry (1971), *The Measurement of Fiscal Policy: An Analysis of Tax Systems in Terms of the Political Distinction between 'Right' and 'Left'*, Confederation of British Industry, London. Now obtainable from the author at 26 Lancaster Court, Banstead, Surrey SM7 1RR.

Bracewell-Milnes, Barry (1974a), *Redistribution in Reverse: More Equal Shares of Wealth Mean Less Equal Shares of Spending*, Aims of Industry, London.

Bracewell-Milnes, Barry (1974b), *Is Capital Taxation Fair? The Tradition and the Truth*, Institute of Directors, London.

Bracewell-Milnes, Barry (1976), 'A Liberal Tax Policy: Tax Neutrality and Freedom of Choice', *British Tax Review*, February. Subsequently reprinted by Libertarian Alliance, London, 1988.

Bracewell-Milnes, Barry (1981), *The Taxation of Industry: Fiscal Barriers to the Creation of Wealth*, Panopticum Press, London.

Bracewell-Milnes, Barry (1982), *Land and Heritage: The Public Interest in Personal Ownership*, Hobart Paper 93, Institute of Economic Affairs, London.

Bracewell-Milnes, Barry (1989), *The Wealth of Giving: Every One in His Inheritance*, Research Monograph 43, Institute of Economic Affairs, London.

Bracewell-Milnes, Barry (1994), *Will to Succeed: Inheritance without Taxation*, Adam Smith Institute, London.

Bracewell-Milnes, Barry (1997), 'The Hidden Costs of Inheritance Taxation', in Guido Erreygers and Toon Vandevelde (eds), *Is Inheritance Legitimate? Ethical and Economic Aspects of Wealth Transfers*, Springer-Verlag, Berlin.

Bresciani-Turroni, Costantino (1909), *Appunti sulla Teoria delle Distribuzioni di Frequenze*, Giornale degli Economisti.

Bresciani-Turroni, Costantino (1916), Review of Gini's *Sulla Misura di Concentrazione*, Giornale degli Economisti.

Dalton, Hugh (1920), 'The Measurement of the Inequality of Incomes', *Economic Journal*, September.

Dalton, Hugh (1925), *Some Aspects of the Inequality of Incomes in Modern Communities*, George Routledge and Sons, London, 1925.

Dunkel, Otto (1909), 'Generalised Geometric Means and Algebraic Equations', *Annals of Mathematics*, October.

Erreygers, Guido (1996), *Early Socialist Thought on Bequest and Inheritance* (paper presented at the 1996 History of Economics Society Conference, University of British Columbia, Vancouver, Canada), mimeo, UFSIA, University of Antwerp, June.

Erreygers, Guido (1997), *Views on Inheritance in the History of Economic Thought*, in Guido Erreygers and Toon Vandevelde (eds), *Is Inheritance Legitimate? Ethical and Economic Aspects of Wealth Transfers*, Springer-Verlag, Berlin.

European Commission (1994a), *Official Journal of the European Communities*, 23 July.

European Commission (1994b), *Official Journal of the European Communities*, 31 December.

European Commission (1998), *Official Journal of the European Communities*, 28 March.

Gini, Corrado (1912), '*Variabilità & Mutabilità*', *Studi Economico-giuridici*, University of Cagliari.

Gini, Corrado (1914), '*Sulla Misura della Concentrazione e della Variabilità dei Caratteri*', *Lettere ed Arti*, Atti del Reale Istituto Veneto di Scienze.

Gini, Corrado (1930), *Sul Massimo degli Indici di Variabilità Assoluta e sulle sue Applicazioni agli Indici di Variabilità Relativa e al Rapporto di Concentrazione*, Metron.

Housman, A. E. (1905), Preface to *The Editing of Juvenal*.

Jouvenel, (Baron) Bertrand de (1951), *The Ethics of Redistribution*, Cambridge University Press, Cambridge.

Kaldor, Nicholas (1942), 'The Income Burden of Capital Taxes', *Review of Economic Studies*, summer. Reprinted in the American Economic Association's *Readings in the Economics of Taxation*, Richard D. Irwin, Inc., Homewood, Illinois, 1959.

Lal, Deepak, and H. Myint (1996), *The Political Economy of Poverty, Equity and Growth*, Clarendon Press, Oxford.

Lorenz, M. O. (1905), 'Methods of Measuring the Concentration of Wealth', *Quarterly Publications of the American Statistical Association*, June.

McCulloch, J. R. (1852), *Taxation*.

Marshall, Alfred (1961), *Principles of Economics*, Macmillan, for the Royal Economic Society, London.

Mises, Ludwig von (1949), *Human Action*, William Hodge, London.

Mortara, Giorgio (1910), '*Metodi Elementari per lo Studio delle Distribuzioni di Caratteri*', *Giornale degli Economisti*.

Orwell, George (1949), *Nineteen Eighty-four*, Martin Secker and Warburg, London.

Persons, Warren M. (1909), 'The Variability in the Distribution of Wealth and Income', *Quarterly Journal of Economics*.

Pietra, Gaetano (1914), '*Delle Relazioni tra gli Indici di Variabilità*', *Lettere ed Arti*, Atti del Reale Istituto Veneto di Scienze, November.

Ricci, Umberto (1915), '*Confronti fra Medie*', *Giornale degli Economisti*, July.

Ricci, Umberto (1916), '*L'Indice di Variabilità e la Curva dei Redditi*', *Giornale degli Economisti*, July.

Rignano, Eugenio, *Un Socialismo in Accordo colla Dottrina Economica Liberale*. J. Stamp's *The Social Significance of the Death Duties* was adapted from the translation of Rignano by Dr Schultz. Rignano's *The Social Significance of the Inheritance Tax* was published in New York by Knopf in 1924.

Rothbard, Murray (1970), *Power and Market: Government and the Economy*, Institute for Humane Studies, Menlo Park, California.

Sandford, C. T. (1965), *Taxing Inheritance and Capital Gains*, Hobart Paper 32, Institute of Economic Affairs, London.

Simons, Henry (1938), *Personal Income Taxation*, University of Chicago Press, Chicago.

Smart, Christopher, *Jubilate Agno*.

Smith, Adam, *The Wealth of Nations*.

Tawney, R. H. (1931), *Equality*, George Allen and Unwin, London.

Watkins, G. P. (1909), 'The Measurement of Concentration of Wealth', *Quarterly Journal of Economics*.

Yntema, Dwight B. (1933), 'Measures of the Inequality in the Personal Distribution of Wealth or Income', *Journal of the American Statistical Association*, December.

Young, Allyn A. (1917), *Do the Statistics of the Concentration of Wealth in the United States Mean What They Are Commonly Assumed to Mean?*, Publications of the American Statistical Association.

Works not cited in this monograph

Allais, Maurice (1977), *L'Impôt sur le Capital et la Réforme Monétaire*, Hermann, Paris.

Barna, T. (1958), 'The Burden of Death Duties in Terms of an Annual Tax', *Review of Economic Studies*, May.

Beach, William W. (2000), *Time to Eliminate the Costly Death Tax*, Executive Memorandum 679, Heritage Foundation, Washington, DC, 2000.

Bhargava, R. N. (1952), *The Principle and Problems of Inheritance Taxation*, Nand Kishore and Brothers, Banaras.

Bijon, S. (1927), *Etude Critique de l'Evolution de l'Impôt de Succession*, Librairie Dalloz, Paris.

Coffield, James (1970), *A Popular History of Taxation*, Longman, London.

Edgens, Jefferson G. (1999), *Bury the Estate Tax for a Truly Sustainable Economy*, Commentary, Georgia Public Policy Foundation, Atlanta, Georgia.

Handy, Albert (1929), *Inheritance and Other Like Taxes*, Prentice-

Hall, New York.

Harriss, C. Lowell (1940), *Gift Taxation in the United States*, American Council on Public Affairs, Washington, DC.

Hodge, Scott A. (2000), *It's Time to Bury the Death Tax*, Capital Comment 283, Citizens for a Sound Economy Foundation, Washington, DC.

Holcomb, A. E. (1925), *Proceedings of National Conference on Inheritance and Estate Taxation*, National Tax Association, New York.

McCaffery, Edward J., and Richard E. Wagner (2000), *A declaration of independence from death taxation: a bipartisan appeal*, Public Interest Institute, Mt Pleasant, Iowa, July.

Sandford, C. T. (1971), *Taxing Personal Wealth: an Analysis of Capital Taxation in the United Kingdom – History, Present Structure and Future Possibilities*, Allen and Unwin, London.

Schultz, W. J. (1926), *The Taxation of Inheritance*, Houghton Mifflin, New York.

Shoup, Carl S. (1966), *Federal Estate and Gift Taxes*, Brookings Institution, Washington, DC.

Smith, R. S. (1993), *Personal Wealth Taxation: Canadian Tax Policy in a Historical and an International Setting*, Canadian Tax Foundation, Toronto.

Tait, Alan A. (1967), *The Taxation of Personal Wealth*, University of Illinois Press, Urbana, London.

Tolley (2000/01a), *Business and Agricultural Property Relief*.

Tolley (2000/01b), *Estate Planning*.

Tolley (2000/01c), *Inheritance Tax*.

Vickrey, William (1972), *Agenda for Progressive Taxation*, Augustus M. Kelley, Clifton.

Wagner, Richard E. (1973), *Death and Taxes*, American Enterprise

Institute for Public Policy Research, Washington, DC.

Wagner, Richard E. (1977), *Inheritance and the State*, American Enterprise Institute for Public Policy Research, Washington, DC.

West, Max (1908), *The Inheritance Tax*, Columbia University Press, New York.

ABOUT THE IEA

The Institute is a research and educational charity (No. CC 235 351), limited by guarantee. Its mission is to improve understanding of the fundamental institutions of a free society with particular reference to the role of markets in solving economic and social problems.

The IEA achieves its mission by:

- a high-quality publishing programme
- conferences, seminars, lectures and other events
- outreach to school and college students
- brokering media introductions and appearances

The IEA, which was established in 1955 by the late Sir Antony Fisher, is an educational charity, not a political organisation. It is independent of any political party or group and does not carry on activities intended to affect support for any political party or candidate in any election or referendum, or at any other time. It is financed by sales of publications, conference fees and voluntary donations.

In addition to its main series of publications the IEA also publishes a quarterly journal, *Economic Affairs*, and has two specialist programmes – Environment and Technology, and Education.

The IEA is aided in its work by a distinguished international Academic Advisory Council and an eminent panel of Honorary Fellows. Together with other academics, they review prospective IEA publications, their comments being passed on anonymously to authors. All IEA papers are therefore subject to the same rigorous independent refereeing process as used by leading academic journals.

IEA publications enjoy widespread classroom use and course adoptions in schools and universities. They are also sold throughout the world and often translated/reprinted.

Since 1974 the IEA has helped to create a world-wide network of 100 similar institutions in over 70 countries. They are all independent but share the IEA's mission.

Views expressed in the IEA's publications are those of the authors, not those of the Institute (which has no corporate view), its Managing Trustees, Academic Advisory Council members or senior staff.

Members of the Institute's Academic Advisory Council, Honorary Fellows, Trustees and Staff are listed on the following page.

The Institute gratefully acknowledges financial support for its publications programme and other work from a generous benefaction by the late Alec and Beryl Warren.

For information about subscriptions to IEA publications, please contact:

Subscriptions
The Institute of Economic Affairs
2 Lord North Street
London SW1P 3LB

Tel: 020 7799 8900
Fax: 020 7799 2137
Website: www.iea.org.uk/books/subscribe.htm

Other papers recently published by the IEA include:

WHO, What and Why?

Transnational Government, Legitimacy and the World Health Organization
Roger Scruton
Occasional Paper 113; ISBN 0 255 36487 3
£8.00

The World Turned Rightside Up

A New Trading Agenda for the Age of Globalisation
John C. Hulsman
Occasional Paper 114; ISBN 0 255 36495 4
£8.00

The Representation of Business in English Literature

Introduced and edited by Arthur Pollard
Readings 53; ISBN 0 255 36491 1
£12.00

Anti-Liberalism 2000

The Rise of New Millennium Collectivism
David Henderson
Occasional Paper 115; ISBN 0 255 36497 0
£7.50

Capitalism, Morality and Markets

Brian Griffiths, Robert A. Sirico, Norman Barry & Frank Field
Readings 54; ISBN 0 255 36496 2
£7.50

A Conversation with Harris and Seldon

Ralph Harris & Arthur Seldon
Occasional Paper 116; ISBN 0 255 36498 9
£7.50

Malaria and the DDT Story

Richard Tren & Roger Bate
Occasional Paper 117; ISBN 0 255 36499 7
£10.00

A Plea to Economists Who Favour Liberty: Assist the Everyman

Daniel B. Klein
Occasional Paper 118; ISBN 0 255 36501 2
£10.00

Waging the War of Ideas
John Blundell
Occasional Paper 119; ISBN 0 255 36500 4
£10.00

The Changing Fortunes of Economic Liberalism
Yesterday, Today and Tomorrow
David Henderson
Occasional Paper 105 (new edition); ISBN 0 255 36520 9
£12.50

The Global Education Industry
Lessons from Private Education in Developing Countries
James Tooley
Hobart Paper 141 (new edition); ISBN 0 255 36503 9
£12.50

Saving Our Streams
The Role of the Anglers' Conservation Association in Protecting English and Welsh Rivers
Roger Bate
Research Monograph 53; ISBN 0 255 36494 6
£10.00

Better Off Out?

The Benefits or Costs of EU Membership
Brian Hindley & Martin Howe
Occasional Paper 99 (new edition); ISBN 0 255 36502 0
£10.00

Buckingham at 25

Freeing the Universities from State Control
Edited by James Tooley
Readings 55; ISBN 0 255 36512 8
£15.00

Lectures on Regulatory and Competition Policy

Irwin M. Stelzer
Occasional Paper 120; ISBN 0 255 36511 X
£12.50

Misguided Virtue

False Notions of Corporate Social Responsibility
David Henderson
Hobart Paper 142; ISBN 0 255 36510 1
£12.50

HIV and Aids in Schools
The Political Economy of Pressure Groups and Miseducation
Barrie Craven, Pauline Dixon, Gordon Stewart & James Tooley
Occasional Paper 121; ISBN 0 255 36522 5
£10.00

The Road to Serfdom
The Reader's Digest *condensed version*
Friedrich A. Hayek
Occasional Paper 122; ISBN 0 255 36530 6
£7.50

Bastiat's *The Law*
Introduction by Norman Barry
Occasional Paper 123; ISBN 0 255 36509 8
£7.50

A Globalist Manifesto for Public Policy
Charles Calomiris
Occasional Paper 124; ISBN 0 255 36525 X
£7.50